MY
DARK COUNTRY

My Dark Country
A culture of violence

Danelle Murray

My Dark Country – A culture of violence
ISBN Number 978-0-9991164-6-3

Danelle Murray asserts the moral right to be identified as the author of this work in accordance with the UK Copyright, Designs and Patents Act 1988.
© Arcanum Press Ltd 2019

All rights reserved. No part of this publication may be reproduced, stored in a retrieval system, or transmitted, in any form by any means, electronic, mechanical, photocopying or otherwise, except as permitted by the U.K. Copyright, Designs and Patents Act 1988, without the prior permission of the publisher.

First published in 2017 by Danelle Murray. Second edition published in 2019 by Arcanum Press.

Arcanum Press LLC is registered in the State of Kansas, United States of America, entity number 8681348.
Arcanum Press Ltd is registered in England & Wales, company number 10704825

I will love the light for it shows me the way, yet I will endure the darkness for it shows me the stars.
Og Mandino, Author

PROLOGUE

There is no clear beginning to my life story, only those moments that I remember. Nor is there a clear way of telling in which way it will end. There are only dreams and hopeful predictions.

Writing this book proved a difficult task, partly because remembering meant reliving those moments in time I spent many hours, days and even years trying to forget. I have guarded these experiences for many years, afraid of the pain the recollections would bring ... and partly because of the honesty it required.

Life is nothing more than a collection of personal perceptions. It is not what happened to us that is of importance, but rather how we view these experiences and how they fit into our 'self' - the person we have become because of them. The outward experiences - those governed by others and by my physical environment - have long become insignificant to me. The only thing that I value now is my introspective reality and my own view of the world around me.

To those who contributed to my life story, or were affected by the same events, things may have seemed different and their recollections of these memories may be dissimilar to mine. In some cases, I have changed their names for the purpose of this book, to protect their individual identity. In every other respect, the events discussed in this book are all true or, at the very least, my own 'truth'.

Thank you to my beautiful children, Spencer and Rebecca, for giving me a reason to live and to fight for the life you both deserve. At times when I felt that there was no strength left within me, you helped me to see the wonder in this world through your eyes. And to Brendan, my loving husband, who has supported me throughout this process. You are my kindred soul, who understands me better than anyone. Thank you for always being right by my side. All three of you are the bright stars in my darkest of nights.

Thank you to my parents, Renè and Hendrik Dames, for raising me in a loving home and for doing what you could to protect me from harm.

To all my family and friends, thank you for being a part of my life story.

In loving memory of Frank Farrar Bok.

CHAPTER 1

There are some things in life that will stay with you until the day you die. Some things you cannot forget. It becomes a part of your makeup. It defines you, moulds you and sometimes even consumes you. This is my autobiographical memory of experiences that will stay with me forever.

It is 2am on a cold Saturday morning in May. In the faint distance is the sound of jackal calling. We are warming up around the campfire in the boma, discussing the high incidences of crime and violence in our beloved country. Belinda tells a story of her boss' brother who was shot and killed in an armed robbery at his home 2 weeks ago, while Andre adds more logs to the fire. Nicky lost most of her possessions when her house was burgled in December, while she was out visiting family. In turn, we each have a story to share. It is not a pleasant conversation and cold shivers are passing down my spine; it was brought on by a new incident. We have just been hit again. This is the third time in only two months that we have been burgled. We've only been here for a short while and specifically moved here to get away from all the crime. Brendan and I have agreed not to mention anything about the previous occurrences. It is not good for business.

Belinda had woken us at 12:30 am with the phone call: "They took our cellphones, they took the kid's bicycles, guitars.... everything... it's all gone!" We immediately jump out of bed, carry the kids to the car and rush over to the camp that was robbed. Belinda and her friends are guests staying over in our lodge.

Brendan, Bryan and Deon are out looking for the robbers. Deon's iPhone has been taken and we can trace the location of it with software from a website that picks up the GPS coordinates of the device. I'm following their movements on my laptop from the lodge and phoning Brendan with updates. Bryan is in a separate vehicle. The moment he heard what had happened, he raced off in his bakkie to the garage on the corner, to ask if anyone there had spotted guys with bicycles.

"You mean *those* guys?" the petrol attendant says, while pointing at three guys making their way down the road. A large-built man in his mid-30s, riding a small, pink bicycle, carrying a guitar and a cooler bag that is filled with the meat that Bianca had packed for their camp, does look rather suspicious. Bryan aims straight for the offender, but he leaps off the bike and escapes into the veld.
Bryan is able to recover some of the stolen goods.

As I walk around to look at the mess that's been left behind, I suddenly realise that Spencer's bicycle also has been taken. I remember him telling me that he'd lent it to one of the children earlier that day. We hadn't locked it away in the container, as we'd done every other night. Spencer's bicycle is his most prized possession, but he is a soft and generous soul and doesn't mind sharing. He counted off the days to his 6th birthday, waiting for the day his bike would arrive. It has been kept safe at my parents' house for the last year and a bit but, when we moved here, we thought it would be safe enough to bring it over. My mom and dad have a big walk-in safe at their home and an impressive alarm-system. They have been spared from break-ins for the last few years and, fortunately, have been sheltered from the anguish since the incident of 1992. On our last farm, close to Lanseria Airport, nothing was safe and we kept most of our valuables at my parents' home. The farm was located between the Diepsloot informal settlement and a small squatter camp known as Malatjie. The property was right on the Jukskei River and two-thirds of the land had river frontage. This made it impossible to secure the farm with a fence, and it was often used by locals as a pass-through between the two informal areas, Diepsloot to Malatjie.

Like savages, the burglars had indulged in festivities at the bar before they'd left with all the goods. There are food items scattered everywhere; half-drunk bottles of alcohol and vomit on the counter. They ate and drank until their systems couldn't take it anymore and then got sick. They sorted through the bags and took the most valuable items with them. The rest is left dispersed on the floor.

The stolen device leads us straight to a shack in an informal settlement, approximately 7 kilometres from the lodge.

"You are right on their trail; they are right there", I'm busy explaining. Suddenly, I hear a woman's scream and my whole body goes cold and jittery. "I have to run, the kids, I heard a scream", I utter over the phone to Brendan, while jumping onto the quad bike.

Kerry is looking over at the kids, who are asleep in the back of the Land Rover. I'm terrified that it may be Kerry screaming for help. Brendan also stops right in his tracks and turns around to rush home. Kerry and the kids are fine. Rebecca wakes up crying and confused but, within a few minutes, falls asleep again. Later, the cops join the hunt. They are taken to the house where the last activity on the device was recorded. The next morning, the detectives ask to be taken to the same spot. They are speaking Tswana, so it is not possible to follow the whole conversation, but the name 'Thomas' is mentioned a few times. Deon is with them. The shack is inaccessible and secured with a chain and a lock. No one is home, but the detectives are able to speak to a neighbour. She confirms what they suspect and speaks English, so that Deon can also understand.

"It's Thomas who lives here", she says, "I haven't seen him today". Thomas is a repeat offender and the detectives know him well. He operates within a gang of six other felonious men.

"We have arrested him a few times. There is still a warrant out for his arrest".

We are fighting a silent war. There is talk of freedom, but we are not free. We live in unceasing fear that is crippling and a lifestyle of incarceration. We live insecure, behind high walls and burglar bars, not knowing what the future will bring. Every night may be our last.

Two weeks earlier, we were robbed. They walked straight into the room where Kerry and Bryan were sleeping and took their laptops. They broke into Frank's home and stole most of his tool collection. Bryan, Kerry and Frank all live on the property with us. Bryan and Frank moved with us when we left the previous farm. Kerry is employed by us to help with the owls. Bryan does our conservation education and Frank is responsible for maintenance. We all thought that we could escape the dangerous lifestyle we had become so accustomed to, but detested. We were convinced that we would be safe here but are left disheartened by the fallacy we were made to believe. When we looked at buying, we were told that it was a peaceful area and the previous owner hadn't had any trouble for the past 15 years. This was the promise that I made my kids: "There are no more baddies here".

Now, my heart is pounding, my stomach is in a knot and I'm trembling and emotional. We took a big financial risk when we bought the lodge, but I did it for my children. They deserve a better life, one without unceasing fear. It is our responsibility to protect them. We bought the bush lodge through a Deed of Sale agreement. It was a bold move, but the property was ideal for rehabilitating and releasing the owls. And what was even better, the lodge could generate enough income to support our cause. We could host volunteers and students; our members could come and visit and even stay over. At the time, we believed that all our dreams had come true. We knew that it would place a lot of pressure on Brendan and me, because the monthly instalment would be five times higher than a normal bond, but it would be worth it. We wouldn't mind the hard work; it would all pay off in the end.

As I sit staring into the flames, hoping to find an answer, the tears stream down my cheeks. I try not to let anyone notice and walk over to the Landy, where the kids are still fast asleep and oblivious to the reality around them. I glance through the window and see the innocence in their little faces. *Tomorrow, when Spencer wakes up I'll have to tell him about his bicycle. And then I must get my mind right; I cannot afford to become despondent now.* The very fact that we were able to buy this place was a miracle in itself, especially given the long financial struggle we'd endured after Rebecca's birth and taking on the rescue work. We were lucky. Roger was desperate to sell and was willing to accept our terms. A bank would never have given us a loan. I have no option but to make the best of the situation.

CHAPTER 2

I grew up on a smallholding, in a little suburb called Poortview. The primary school I attended was a rural, Afrikaans school, with just over two hundred students. It was a conservative farm school, rich with an Afrikaans culture and belief system. We dressed in an informal green and yellow school uniform and could go to school barefoot for most months of the year. Most of my classmates belonged to the same Christian Church and it was like they were all made from the same mould. They did not differ much from one another in their views and opinions on day-to-day matters and they all seemed to think along the same lines when it came to things in our young milieu. Even though I had many friends, I always felt a bit like an outsider, like I didn't quite fit in.

My parents are religious and raised me to believe in God, but we belonged to a different church than the other kids in my class and had a more liberal outlook on life. Being different meant being wrong - all the time. I remember once receiving an instruction from my Grade 1 teacher to create a self-portrait. As the only southpaw in the class, I was made to feel awkward amongst my peers. The other kids gazed in confusion every time I turned my page at an angle comfortable for me to write or draw. My pages and books were always laid out in front of me at a ninety-degree angle. I proudly coloured my self-portrait, feeling a sense of selfesteem and approval at what I had created. I lightly tinted the white page with a soft orange hue to reflect my pale complexion. My schoolmarm teacher, in view of the whole class, expressed her dissatisfaction. Apparently, what I did not know is that all people had to be coloured using a yellow crayon. Not orange, not pink, but yellow.

Everyone looked at me like I had just been convicted of some heinous crime. Each, in turn, gave me a silent stare. I couldn't understand why I was the only person there who could see that my skin resembled a light orange-pink colour rather than a yellow one. It wasn't so much that they could not see it but, rather, that they had been taught to conform. There was no room for individuality back then. Creativity was looked upon almost as sin. I was devastated and felt insulted. Drawing was the inner sanctum to my personality. It gave reason to my identity. It was the one thing I knew how to do well, the one thing that I believed I was good at. I was never athletic.

I was not an academic. Nor was I a candidate for class leader. These inadequacies made me insecure. The gawkiness of my youth was enforced by my unusually skinny frame, my knobby knees and pixie-shaped ears. But I knew that I could draw better than most of them and, if I wanted to colour my pictures orange, or brown for that matter, then that is what I would do. I am sensitive, but stubborn at the same time.

I've always been introverted and reserved. I shy away from any attention on me. But when I feel it matters, I'll speak my mind. Especially when it comes to something I care about; something I believe in. It is like a flame is lit inside me and it burns through my core. I have to speak up; I cannot let it be. For that moment, I have the uncharacteristic confidence to stand up and be heard.

There are certain things I feel strongly about, things I will not tolerate: I do not like people who oppress others. I do not like people who think they are above others. And I certainly don't like it when people generalise.

It is 16 March 1992, the day before the Referendum of South Africa, the last all-white election the country will ever have. It's been 2 years since President F.W. de Klerk first announced, in his opening address to parliament, that the ban on political parties such as the African National Congress and the South African Communist Party would be lifted and that Nelson Mandela would be released from prison after serving 27 years behind bars. F.W. de Klerk proposed that the apartheid system, initially implemented in 1948, be brought to an end. "The time to negotiate has arrived," the State President announced to the Nation in his powerful speech on the 2nd of February 1990. The Referendum was a simple 'yes' or 'no' election, in which electors indicated their support for the reform process and approval of the negotiations that had started in 1990, a movement to end apartheid in South Africa.

The Referendum that is to take place the very next day is the topic of discussion at school. I'm only eight years old, but am already a passionate activist for human rights. I proudly announce to all my friends that both my parents will be voting 'yes'. I remember feeling ashamed that my own racial group could treat another racial group with such disrespect; I didn't want to be a part of it and was relieved that it was all coming to an end. I would always support the oppressed. My greatgrandfather had fled Poland in the early 1900s to escape the brutality and injustice that was being done to the Jewish folk back then; I couldn't bear my own kind's exploitation of another race. I have empathy for those who suffer and feel their pain as if it were my own. A few friends disagreed with me and mimicked what they had been taught in their bigoted family homes. Some were absolutely terrified of change, and rumours of communism were used by parties such as the Conservative Party (CP), Afrikaner Resistance Movement (AWB) and the Reformed National Party (HNP) to instil fear in voters. Betsie and Mina, our domestic workers, and David and Lucky, our gardeners, were like extended family in our home. They all had African names but had chosen English names to make it easier for us to pronounce. Mina would often plait my hair for school and Betsie helped Mom with the cooking. David had two children who also lived with us, Boniswa and Bongi. Boniswa was only a year younger than me and we played together every day after school. I was colour-blind and knew little about the apartheid regime. I cared for Boniswa and she cared for me. They had a neat home on our property which my dad, who was a property developer, built especially so that they would have a comfortable place to live, close to work, with four spacious rooms, a communal kitchen and two bathrooms. My mother gave them her first-ever owned diningroom set, which was still in neat condition, as furniture in the kitchen. The rooms were fitted with beds and even their linen was provided.

At 8pm, 17 March 1992, a chilling noise passes through the house. It is a school night so I'm already in bed by this time, but I'm listening curiously to hear what will be said in The News that is about to come on TV. The referendum resulted in a 68.6 per cent vote in favour of the motion, signalling the start of a New South Africa. I sit upright in my bed and try to make sense of what I've just heard. It sounded like my mother's voice, but she sounded distressed. My little brother of six shares my room with me, afraid to sleep too far away from my parents. [The family home I grew up in was built by my dad, who was in the construction industry his whole life before retirement. This was a skill that had been passed onto him by my grandfather. The house was designed by the same architect whom my dad had used on most of his projects. It was a rather large, single-level house (my parents considered a house with many stairs to be impractical), built on a twohectare property. The bedrooms were spaced far apart, separated by long passages and living spaces. My room was right next to that of my parents, which is why my younger brother had decided to share with me for a few years.]

"Simon, did you hear that? Go and see what mom and dad are doing?"

I didn't tell him what I'd heard and wasn't quite sure myself if I had misinterpreted the sound. I feel unsettled anyway and call on my younger brother to perform this task about which I feel so uneasy. My brother gets up to go and look but, before he can reach the bedroom door, he is interrupted by uninvited strangers. Two armed men enter my bedroom with our mother. A firearm is pointed in my direction and I am told to get out of bed. We are ordered to lie flat on the floor, next to my bed, facing the ground. The initial few seconds pass, almost in slow motion, as if my mind is trying to make sense of what is happening. *Why are these unfamiliar men in my bedroom?*

"Lie down!" I get the command again, with a cold muzzle tightly pressed against my neck. My heart is racing and I feel a bit weak, almost like I want to faint. My mom begs with our assailants to take us to my sister's room, so the four of us can all be together. My sister is still obliviously asleep in her bed at this point. Her room is down the passage from mine, towards the left wing of the house. My mom fears that the men will find her on her own and that she won't be there to protect her. She would protect us with her own life.

My sister is 11 years old at the time of the attack; she'll be 12 in two months' time. Dornè is a smallframed, timidly-built and fair-skinned blonde girl, with glistening green eyes. Despite her fragile appearance, she is a tower of strength. In relation to myself and my siblings, she is headstrong and uncompromising. She is inherently stubborn and this often lands her in trouble. My mother and my sister are very alike in many ways and Dornè often mothers my younger brother and me.

We are ordered to get up from the floor and are taken to my sister's room. The armed robbers are tense and become increasingly aggressive. Another two are with my dad, on the far side of the house. As we walk, I pray. I pray that my dad is unharmed. I am Daddy's little girl. He is my whole world, my beginning and my end. The worst possible thoughts are passing through my mind. As we arrive in my sister's room, my little brother finds it hard to contain his emotional distress and starts to sob. At six, he hardly knows how to cope with the ordeal and wants only to return to his bed. He is tired, scared and bewildered. The robbers have absolutely no compassion for anyone, not even a young child. The most brutal of the attackers, with hatred-filled eyes, kicks in the direction of my baby brother to silence him, but my mother manages to break the impact with her arm.

"Where is the money!" he shouts at my mother, in a raspy aggressive voice, beating and kicking her, while we look-on, terror-stricken and distressed, until she collapses on the ground.

My sister comes to my mother's defence and, without hesitation, yells out: "She told you, there is no money, now leave her alone!"

His attention is now turned onto my sister. He walks over to her, pressing the gun against her head. "Shut up or I kill you." His eyes are dark and cold. They seem lifeless and hard. The sclera of his eyes is yellow and dull, not white, which makes his appearance evil.

I am sitting tightly-pressed against my sister, sideby-side on her bed, with our shoulders touching. The events playing out seem unreal and it feels like I'm watching from elsewhere, like watching a horror movie play out, or a bad dream. I sit quietly and observe. I am both silenced and numbed by fear. I am dazed and disorientated. The events play out inside a bubble in my head. Even though I am completely capable of seeing and hearing what is going on, I have somehow removed myself from it, as if my body is no longer connected to my mind. My mother is taken away. The robbers lock us inside my sister's room.

"If you try anything, we will kill all of you," are the words we are left with.

The robbers had a considerable amount of information about our family and about the house. They knew about the walk-in safe in my dad's study, which was hidden behind what looked like a wood cupboard. They knew that my elder brother visited every other night and checked with my dad to see if he was expecting him. Michael, a halfbrother on my dad's side, lived with my grandmother at the time. Michael routinely came to visit almost every night around 8pm on his way home from work. He was completing his Bachelors of Commerce Degree through Rand Afrikaans University and had an exam that week, which made him decide to go straight home this particular night. The robbers knew things that were impossible to know from the outside. They had a key to the backdoor. This is how they had entered the house. Nothing was broken; they simply opened the gate with a remote, unlocked the door to our home and walked straight in.

I can hear crying and screaming. I can hear my parents begging their attackers. Again, I start praying.

My sister picks up her Bible from her bedside table and reads to us from the book of Isaiah, "Fear not, for I am with you; be not dismayed, for I am your God; I'll strengthen you, I'll help you, I'll uphold you with my righteous right hand."

The words repeat in my head: "Fear not, for I am with you." I squeeze my left hand as if I am grasping God's hand. Whenever I'm afraid of little thing in life, like going to school for the first time, I feel better holding my dad's hand. With him not here, I try to imagine that God is holding my hand, instead. *Please God, just get us through this. Please God, keep my mommy and daddy safe.*

My mother is returned, but she is covered in blood this time. We are commanded to walk down the passage to the guest bathroom. My dad is already there. *Thank you God*, I shoot up a quick prayer. My hand is still in the same clasped position. I now feel closer to God in this, as if He is there with us. I imagine that by grasping onto His imaginary hand, I have His full attention on us.

We are locked inside the bathroom, and given another warning, "Try anything, and we will come back to kill you!" From the entrance of the bathroom, one cannot see the small corner window that is in a slight indent in the wall.

The robbers must have believed that there was no way for us to get out other than by breaking down the door. My dad slowly opens the window, careful not to make a sound. The threatening command they left us with makes me uneasy and I beg my dad not to do anything until we are sure that they have left.

"Look at your mother," he says. "She needs to get to a doctor."

I look up at my mom and her white T-shirt, with its colourful,]diamond-stud-design, is stained red with blood. Her hand has been badly cut in a struggle with one of the attackers. Three of the men were armed with guns, but one carried a knife. One tried to rape my mother, but she fought him off. For a moment, she had won the struggle and even managed to take the weapon away from one of the robbers, but she feared that he would command the others to harm us and she handed it back to him. Her earrings have been ripped out of her ears. Both my mom and dad's faces are badly bruised and you can even see a shoe imprint in their discoloured skin.

"Okay, but we have to be careful." My dad slowly helps me through the window.

My mother is taken to hospital for treatment and stitches. We spend the rest of the night with the Roets family, who live a few streets down from our house. Talita Roets and my sister are in the same grade and in the same class. Talita's mother takes us to school in the morning. With everything that happened the night before, we arrive a bit late and I must explain the reason for my tardiness to Ms Drienie Kruger.

The whole class stares at me in horror as I blurt out the words: "Men with guns attacked us. They came into our home last night and robbed us."

I can see by the confounded expression on her face that she immediately has regretted her insensitive, stern questioning. These things were still uncommon and unheard of back then.

CHAPTER 3

For weeks, we didn't return home. We stayed with my grandmother. My mother couldn't face being reminded of that horrific night by going back to the surroundings where it all had happened. My dad would return to the house from time to time to check on things and to bring us more clothes or necessities. He never took us with him.

About three days after the incident, my dad is unable to open the gate with his remote. He had changed all the batteries for the gate remotes only a few days before the robbery and they shouldn't be flat so soon. As he opens to check the remote, he notices that the brand of battery now in the remote is different to the one with which he'd recently replaced the old ones. Someone has swapped the remotes. Someone has taken our gate remote, probably to retrieve the code, and replaced it with another. This confirms what my parents had already suspected. Someone assisted the robbers and gave them access to our home. Someone who themselves had access. My mother had given Betsie and Mina a key to the backdoor, so that they could come in early to start their daily cleaning routines. A key had been used by the robbers to open our backdoor and to enter our home on the night of the attack.

Of the four robbers, only one had worn a balaclava to hide his face. The other three were unconcerned about possibly being recognised. It is nearly impossible to identify an attacker, and one is greatly susceptible to distortion when giving an eyewitness account after one has gone through a traumatic experience - unless you already know your attacker. My mother recognised the voice of the fourth robber. He was less aggressive towards her and my father during the attacks; at times, he even intervened to mitigate the severe, hostile behaviour of the others. David was in the house with the three other men that night. David had masked his face, but he couldn't mask his posture and gestures and he certainly couldn't mask his voice. He was armed with a knife and the other three men had guns.

Betsie, Mina, David and Lucky were all arrested and taken in for questioning. I heard they were released two days later. I never saw any of them again. And I never saw Boniswa again, either.

I'll never forget what it was like to return home for the first time after the armed robbery. I had missed sleeping in my own bed and missed sunbathing in the warm morning sun that baked the swing chair in front of my window. I could sit there for hours, doodling in my sketchbook. After the attack, the house felt unfamiliar; it was like we had never lived there, like it belonged to someone else. They took our home from us that night, too, a place that used to offer comfort and safety. All the curtains in the house were kept drawn.

This made the rooms cold and the passage seemed longer and darker than I had remembered it.

The big safe door was still open. They had taken my dad's firearms, most of which were an inheritance from my grandfather. They'd taken his Kruger Rand collection and the 18-carat gold watches my parents had bought on a special occasion on one of their trips abroad. My mom's entire jewellery collection had been stolen, including her wedding and engagement rings. The diamond my grandfather had bought my mother to commemorate the birth of my sister, her first child, and the one he'd bought when she announced that she was pregnant with me, only a few months before his passing, were now being sold on the black market somewhere.

That night, I noticed the Barn Owls breeding at the top of the large, brick-built water-tank tower, for the very first time. It was just about to get dark and my mother had asked me to feed our dog outside. I was trembling in fear but would not go against my mother's wishes. My senses were heightened and alert. That is when I noticed a strange hissing sound coming from above the tower. As I looked up, a Barn Owl sat staring at me like an angel watching over me from above. Its face seemed kind, heart-shaped and angelic. The owls were to breed in that tower for many years to come.

As I think back to the eight year old version of me, when I first fell in love with the sight of a Barn Owl who was breeding at the top of the water tower of my childhood home, I can't help but to feel an extraordinary bond and closeness to these unique birds. Never did I think that years later I would be in the unique position to spend my life as an owl protector. I hold a belief that there is a mystical significance in the fact that as an eightyear-old I believed this Barn Owl to be an angel, sent to look over and protect me. This idea was something I created as a coping mechanism to an ordeal I was far too young to process otherwise.

After the incident, my mother did all the housework herself, with some chores passed down to my sister and me. She would never trust anyone in her home after that day. She tried therapy to help her cope with her post-traumatic stress, but she was uncomfortable with the suggested hypnotic therapy that the psychologist, a male in his late 40s, recommended. My mother had trouble trusting anyone at this point and the therapist would not allow my dad to sit in on the hypnotic sessions. I could see the effect this had on my parents. My mother had trouble sleeping at night, so she used to sleep late in the mornings. My dad hated the fact that he hadn't been able to protect his family on the night of the attack, which turned into feelings of guilt and self-recrimination within him. He was never quite the same after that night in March of 1992.

I was exceptionally sensitive as a child. Things affected me differently than other kids. The way in which the robbery affected my parents, affected me too. I could see their pain. I could see their suffering, but there was nothing I could do to change it. I became very religious over the next few years. My parents couldn't protect us from all the evil out there, but maybe God could. I grew fearful of the outside world, i.e. that which did not include family. I viewed it as a dubious place, downright hostile. This inescapable world of darkness was no place for me. I became suspicious of everyone around me. Religion became a way to escape what I felt. God was a symbol of trust, beauty and peace. Every night, before I went to bed, I would read from my Bible, the same verse over and over, until I became calm and could finally close my eyes and dare to fall asleep. I would close my hand in a tight grip, holding onto God. It became easier to sleep after a while and I thought of that terrible incident less and less as time passed. I shied away from anything that represented violence or conflict, even that depicted in animations for children, or fairy tales.

The staff quarters were now occupied by four, young police officers, who worked at the station that covered our area. From time to time, one of them would look into the progress of our case, but crime was on the increase and it became increasingly difficult for the police force to keep the peace. Most cases were pushed aside for other cases - usually more significant cases -

to be investigated. With the cops there, at least we had some protection and perpetrators seemed to pick easier targets. We also adopted Sasha, a one-yearold German Shepherd, who was rejected by the Dog Squad during her training. Sasha followed me everywhere and I felt safer with her around. Sometimes, I overheard the gruesome stories told by the young policemen when they came over for a cup of coffee with my parents. I would run back to my room and think of ways to keep the bad people away; I planned booby traps and designed weapons with which to protect myself.

The same gang of men who attacked us allegedly killed several people in armed robberies that followed, but the police never managed to keep these men behind bars. The thought that they remained out there continuing to rob, rape, assault and murder haunted me for years.

CHAPTER 4

I could hardly contain my excitement when Francie had moved into the big, white house opposite from us with her parents, Cathy and Robert. She was an only child and had two, purebred Rottweilers as companions. Vulcan, the male Rottweiler, was a self-assured, steady and fearless dog, while Sofi, the female Rottweiler, was much more placid in nature and very affectionate towards people. Both dogs demonstrated extraordinary loyalty towards Francie, a quality I admired in them. Dad agreed that we could have one of the puppies and I had hoped that ours would show me the same affection.

After the birth of the pups, we waited another 8 weeks before Bruno could come and live with us. Bruno was a little male Rottie - a perfect specimen, quintessentially proportioned, compact and sturdily build. He had a shiny, black coat, with two brown dots just above each of his eyes. Since Sasha had gone to live with my brother, to companion my Gran's German Shepard, Olk, I had been very lonely and longed for the bond that can only develop between a human and a dog.

Bruno stole my heart from the first day we met. He became my guardian, emotionally more than anything else. He gave me courage to be brave. Bruno was a shadow by my side. I told Bruno all my secrets, my fears and my misgivings. I often told him about the bad men who had come into our house before he was around. We passed the days in the wooden house that Dad had put up in the playarea. In gratitude to him for listening, I evenly shared any chocolates or treats Mom gave me. Bruno gave true meaning to the words 'a man's best friend'.

Bruno never got upset. Even on days when I was sulky, Bruno would be exactly the same. He was a constant in my life, dependable and loyal. I learned a lot from his good character and patience. I would always aspire to show others the same respect that Bruno demonstrated to me. Dogs love unconditionally; they keep no record of what you do wrong. Bruno taught me selfless love. My love for animals developed at a very young age. I preferred them over most human beings. I often imagined myself in the character of Sheena, Queen of the jungle. Sheena was a jungle-girl comiccharacter, first created by Will Eisner and Jerry Iger. Columbia Pictures developed their story into a film in 1984. In my make-believe world, I could communicate with animals. I could spend hours quietly staring at the birds in our garden, or at wild animals in the game reserve we visited every June holiday, pretending that they knew my thoughts. For my 10th birthday, my dad bought me a small microscope, an inexpensive toy that remarkably imitated a professional microscope used by veterinarians. Whenever one of our dogs went to the vet, I would go along and the doctor would allow me to look down the microscope. He'd take the time to explain the parasites and blood cells that were visible. I am sure that he noticed my keen interest to learn more. At home, I would find things in the garden to examine under my own microscope. I often found small birds to rescue. In most cases, they would be baby birds that had fallen from their nests. I enjoyed taking care of them. It gave me a sense of purpose in God's creation.

Growing up, my mother was often abrasive towards me. She got annoyed by my sensitivity, my likeliness to be offended or hurt. I guess she believed that I needed to be stronger to survive in this world. Maybe she just had trouble understanding it, understanding me. She wanted to toughen me up. I grew to resent my ability to feel so intensely. I learned, over the years, to suppress most of my emotions, but I didn't feel the pain of them any less. I believed that this was a weakness in myself, one that I was determined to overcome. I know, without a doubt, that my mother loved me unconditionally and that her intentions were never to hurt me. I understand it now better than ever, since having become a mother myself. In her own way, she tried to protect me and save me from the heartache I would still have to encounter in my life ahead.

I liked that Bruno couldn't judge me for my sensitive nature. We walked great distances, to the far side of the property where the terrain was still covered in bushveld vegetation. Between the kiepersol trees was a large, flat rock, from where I could sit and watch the birds dance. I wasn't scared to be out there, when Bruno was with me.

I have been told that most African people fear black dogs. In Bantu-speaking African cultures, high emphasis is placed on the supernatural and spiritual world, and a cultural belief system is built around this. Africa is a multicultural society, with a high diversity in social norms. There are superstitious beliefs about black dogs; bad things will happen to you if you are bitten by one. This was not a notion in which I myself believed, but Betsie insisted that the folktale was true. She told me many stories about her peoples' belief in the spiritual world. She told me that when people die, they continue life as spirit-beings, who can exercise great power over us.

"We should pay tribute to our ancestral spirits. They live there, where the sun sets," she used to say.

It is believed that these ancestral spirits have great influence over the living and control what happens in their lives. They send either prosperity or misfortune to the ones they have left behind. People like Betsie believe that these spirits should be honoured in ritual performances. She also believes in magic and witchcraft. Natural occurrences that cannot be controlled, yet influence her life and that of her family, like illness, cold weather, wind and rain, are described and understood as the spiritual forces of her ancestors.

These spirits use bodily creatures, such as animals, to exercise control over the living. I found the tales fascinating and listened attentively as she explained.

Even to those who did not share this superstitious belief, Bruno, who was very muscular, appeared rather intimidating, if they were not familiar with his happy-go-lucky temperament. I felt safe and at ease with him around. When Bruno got sick, my whole world came tumbling down. I hated leaving him at the vet. *Will he understand why I couldn't stay?* I cried to my dad and made him promise that Bruno would be okay, that the vet would cure him of whatever was hurting and making him ill. *He probably wants me there to comfort him.*

That afternoon, though, when I came home from school, my dad gently broke the bad news to me: "Bruno is in heaven now."

A few weeks after Bruno's death, several more cases of poisoning in the area came to light. Bromethalin Rodenticide was used to eliminate dogs that could pose a threat to scouting burglars.

Dad slept with his revolver under his pillow. He would always be prepared from now on. We were no longer allowed to play outside after dark. By eight-o-clock each night, the alarm would be set to alert us to any possible intruders. On a few occasions, I would wake up from the warning shots my dad had fired from my bedroom window, where there was the best view over the garden, to chase away men who had come to steal.

Once Bruno was no longer around, I spent more and more time inside my room. I often wished that I could cut myself off from the world, a cruel place where I felt misunderstood. I blocked out everything that made me feel uncomfortable. I could get lost in my thoughts, basking in the sun that shone in through my bedroom window, while drawing and painting pictures of a perfect life.

Sometimes I would put on my brave face to be social, more so during my adolescent years. To people who met me, I seemed normal. I faked confidence, like everyone else, and made an effort to make friends and fit in. This was something that came naturally to Dornè. She had many friends and was popular with most. I had friends too, but it took time before I could open up to someone. I am inherently shy and reserved; qualities that are often misinterpreted as snobbish and unapproachable. Inside myself, I battled with my harrowing world view, an after-effect of the armed robbery that made me mistrustful of people.

I never forgave Mina and Betsie for their betrayal.

CHAPTER 5

I met Brendan on the 4th of January 2006, at the young age of 22. I was still very naive and unworldly, and slightly intimidated by the big age gap between us. Brendan was 33 at the time, 11 years my senior. From the first instance he caught my eye, I found myself intensely intrigued by his mysterious yet confident demeanour. Brendan is a handsome, well-defined man. When we met, he had dark black hair, with only slight streaks of silver-grey in his sideburns and around his ears. His appearance was effortlessly elegant, with that attractive salt-and-pepper look. He was dressed in a pair of blue jeans and a slim-fitting black T-shirt. His eyes were soulful and I could see that he had a life-story good enough to tell. I wanted to read him like the pages of a book. There were secrets behind his contemplative eyes, secrets I yearned to uncover. I smiled back at his stare, like a freshlyblossomed flower, ready for his picking.

Brendan was an acquaintance of Ilse, a close friend of mine who has a perceptive ability to tell when people are a suitable match for each other. She knew it would be a good idea to introduce us.

Brendan asked me out for coffee and we spent hours talking and sharing our thoughts. We were both instantly attracted to each other by our discernible likenesses. I found some of his behaviour a bit peculiar at first, but understood that he was too old to waste his time on another insignificant love-affair that wouldn't go anywhere. He was too much of a gentleman for that.

Brendan has a foot-fetish and after about an hour in conversation, he promptly dived under the table to check if my feet met his requirements. I thought it strange, but honest. I told him about my interest in criminology and we discovered that we shared a keen interest in human behaviour. Brendan had been a cop in his early career and said that he had seen disturbing things while employed by the police force.

At first, Brendan was selective with the details of his life that he chose to make known to me. He was emotionally cautious and I could tell that he had been hurt by someone in his past. Brendan didn't trust easily when it came to affairs of the heart. When we met, he was a free-spirited soul, constrained by the woes of the world. In his ideal life, he would choose to live somewhere on an island, unaffected by everyday pressure and not concerned about anything other than the weather. He was a loner, easily satisfied with his own company. He would visit Inhaca Island in Mozambique four times a year to escape his busy lifestyle. Brendan owned a rustic camp on the island, where he entertained small groups of people from time to time.

Brendan had been married before, to Nikki, with whom he shares two children, Shayne and Skye. They had been divorced for seven years when I met him. Brendan hesitated to tell me about his kids at first, worried that I may have been overwhelmed by the complications and responsibilities of his life. I only met his family months after our acquaintanceship.

When he finally found the courage to be truthful and disclose intimate aspects of his life to me, the pride of being a father became apparent in his responses. Skye, his daughter, was 7 at the time. He spoke about her all the time. She was considered in his every notion.

"Skye would love this place; she can get so excited about all these little things." His eyes would light up as he explained her flamboyant character. "Skye is fascinated by gemstones, she has a collection of books about it," he would boast.

I got to know Skye long before I met her. Brendan loves Shayne just the same, but he finds it harder to relate to Shayne's specific interests. They have little in common and their viewpoints often differ. Shayne is Brendan's first-born and is seven years older than Skye. "He is a good boy, with a good heart." When he speaks of Shayne, there is concern in his voice. Brendan had little influence over Shayne's life while he was growing up. He often regretted the fact that Nikki and her parents had not consulted and included him more in the choices they had made for Shayne.

Our relationship developed, unrushed. We took time to get to know each other. We appreciated every moment we spent together, without any expectations as to what would follow. Brendan took me on several dates. During the day, we rode his bike on winding roads to countryside restaurants, where we could quietly sit and share our thoughts. At night, we visited the buzzing, upmarket restaurants along the streets of Melville and Park Town. It was a simple and uncomplicated beginning to our life together. Over the months, our flirtatious love grew into a strong affection for each other. Spending time with Brendan was like discovering a new dimension to my own self.

My parents didn't immediately approve of Brendan. They judged him by what he represented - a divorced, Englishman, with two children, who was over a decade older than me. People tend to sort others in notional boxes, each with a specific label.

"Does that mean that someone who is divorced with kids does not deserve to find love again?" I used to argue. Even my friends found it difficult to accept our relationship. They couldn't understand why I would choose to be with someone who came with what they viewed as burdensome encumbrances. I didn't see it that way. I just saw a good man and a good father, qualities that made me fall even more deeply in love with him. I knew that there would be certain challenges to our relationship. When I decided to share my life with Brendan, I took a cautious decision always to be considerate of his children's needs. They would always come first. I would not let our relationship have any adverse effect on the life of an innocent child. I made a concerted effort to build a good relationship with them. Nikki and I became friends. We spend most significant dates together as a family and have shared many special holidays. It is important to Brendan, and therefore also to me, that Skye and Shayne have both their parents present in all aspects of their lives.

Brendan grew up with a callous father. His father was not a family man, but was admired by acquaintances who didn't know his true character. Brendan's distinct dislike for his own father is probably the reason for his kind approach towards those he meets. He always concerns himself with the troubles of others. He is empathetic and can relate to people's situations. He would never be anything like his own dad.

Brendan's mother often suffered under his dad's rule. Brendan's dad had many mistresses and baseborn children, half-brothers and half-sisters whom Brendan and his brothers had never met. His father could disappear for months at a time and then return in a destructive mood. His actions had a deleterious effect on the family. To this day, Brendan shies away from conflict. He once told me that his dad had tied his dog to a tree and shot it, because it had chased one of the sheep on the farm. Their family home had doors filled with bullet holes. Once, his dad got so angry that he shot a hole through the floorboards, while firmly pressing Brendan down on the ground, pointing the gun next to his ear merely centimetres away from his head. Brendan escaped the unpleasantness through his bedroom window. He spent hours in the veld adjacent to their home. This is where his interest in raptors developed. At the age of twelve, Brendan was already an expert on birds of prey. He observed and studied their hunting and nesting behaviour; he noted every detail, such as habitat and preferred prey. He learnt to know each species well. During his youth, he would often miss school, swapping his school books for a pair of binoculars and his Robert's bird book.

Brendan's dad passed away from cancer a few years before I met him. Brendan's mother, a graceful and feminine woman now in her 70s, never took another man. Jenny was in her early 40s when she separated from her husband for good. She had married Patrick straight out of school and had stayed loyal towards him her whole life. She is an attractive, well-groomed lady and takes pride in her appearance. She probably could have had her pick to men, but chose to remain single after the divorce. I often wonder where she found the strength to raise three boys all on her own. Fortunately, she was spared from knowing the full extent of the mischief they got up to. She raised her sons well. They are all successful in their own ways. To me, she is a warm-hearted mother-in-law. As delicate as she may appear, she is a strong woman who had to withstand years of mistreatment. It is hard to imagine this when you meet her now.

In our marriage today, Brendan and I have a very strong connection, reinforced by our shared experiences. We share much more than just a life together; we share our innermost beings. We respect and support each other in all aspects. Our relationship is successful, with enough passion, a commitment to be faithful to each other and shared intimacy.

"Lucky in love, but unlucky in everything else," Brendan often jests.

CHAPTER 6

On the 7th of January 2007, Brendan phoned me to let me know that he was back from his trip to Mozambique. I was staying in Kim and Alsten's house for the week, to look after their animals while they were on a short holiday at the South coast. A Basset Hound named Mow, an African Grey Parrot and a ginger cat called Caramel were my house companions in the duplex townhouse, in a security complex in Windsor.

"Meet me for dinner."

I'd had time to think about our relationship while Brendan was away and I wanted to talk to him about things that were bothering to me. I thought that it was time for us to be more open about our lives. I wanted to get to know his family and other significant people in his life. He was still, after a year of dating, living a large part of his life without me. I welcomed his suggestion to meet for dinner.
It was the perfect opportunity to talk.

We did talk over dinner, but Brendan has a way of avoiding personal matters. After a pleasant supper, he walks me over to my car and opens the door for me. As we're taking our leave of each other, he leans over to kiss me.

"I'm still not sure that you understand what I was trying to tell you." I take a step back to let him know that I'm serious about my request. I smile and tell him to think about what I've said.

At that moment, a man dressed in dark clothing, with a heavy jacket, approaches us. Brendan and I are both still standing at the door of my car. I do not immediately hear what he is asking and I assume that he is begging when he asks for money.

"I'm sorry, we can't help you. We don't have cash on us."

"This is an armed robbery," the man says, but once again I do not register what he is trying to tell us. This time, I assume that he is warning us about an armed robbery that is taking place at the garage, which is not far from where we are parked. I make this assumption because of his uniform, mistaking him as the security-guard on duty at the filling station. Garages are often targeted by robbers, especially after dark. My brain is refusing to accept the reality of what is taking place. Naively, I don't expect a complete stranger to want to cause us any harm. The idea does not fit into my social framework, so my brain refuses to process the information. I must seem witless to the robber. He has to repeat himself three times before I react accordingly.

On his third request, he responds in an aggressive tone: "This is an armed robbery!" He takes his hand out of his jacket pocket to show us that he is armed with a 9mm handgun. He grabs my handbag and pushes me onto my car seat. He starts going through the bag and shouts that he wants money. He takes out my phone and places it in his pocket.

"I don't carry cash, only cards," I respond.

"Come with me!" the man demands.

I fight him. "I refuse to go anywhere with you!" I yell in response. At that moment, I look back at the garage and an old, red, VW sedan is parked there, with two other men sitting inside, one in the driver's seat and one in the back. The vehicle is dinged and discoloured and looks unroadworthy. The back door is open and they have Brendan in the back seat, with a gun pointing at his head.
"Get in!" comes the second command.

Brendan tries to calm me, fearing that the man will hurt me if I protest too much. "It will be okay; they just want money, then they will let us be. We are going to an ATM to draw cash." I hesitantly get into the car. The assailant follows. Brendan and I are now wedged between two guys, each armed with a gun. A third aggressor is driving the car and I soon realise that we are not traveling in the direction of any banks.

"Where are you taking us?" Why are we not going to the ATM like you said?" I anxiously question. The attacker next to me hits me with the back of his hand holding the firearm and tells me to be quiet. The driver threatens that they will kill us if I'm 'cheeky' like that again. My phone is passed to me and I'm forced to enter our pin codes for our bank accounts on the phone. We are questioned about the amount of money that is available in either account.

"That's not enough!" the driver shouts. "You are lying to us. We know that you have money. You whites all have money! Where are you hiding it?" he demands, irate. The driver pulls over onto a gravel road that leads into a veld.

"We really don't have anything more to offer you," I plead with the men. "I only earn a small salary, enough to pay for my monthly expenses."

"Shut up! Shut up and get out!" the driver shouts.

We are shoved out of the vehicle and ordered to walk in the direction of complete darkness. It is about 8pm on a Sunday night.

"Where are we going?" I question again. A gun is pointed at each of our heads as we are marched along.

The attackers are now taunting, crabbing at me. They hit Brendan when he comes to my defence. The car drives off and we are left behind with two of the men. My head is spinning, as different thoughts enter my mind. I do not want my parents to wake up to the news that the police have found my body somewhere on a deserted piece of land.

Brendan and I try and keep as close to each other as our captors will allow.

"What if they try to rape me?" I whisper to Brendan in terror. One of the assailants is more perverse than the other. I get the impression that he is on some sort of substance, a mood-altering drug. His behaviour is abnormal. He seems to derive pleasure from the torment we are experiencing. His facial expressions read as someone who is amused.

"You have to make yourself sick. Put your finger down your throat if you must. It will discourage any sexual notions."

We are told to sit down and wait. They are expecting a call from the driver to inform them that the money withdrawal has been made. Neither of the attackers are wearing anything to cover their faces. This makes me more nervous. They are not making any attempt to hide their identities.

Brendan tries to negotiate with the two men. He tells them that he has money hidden and that he will take them to go and collect it, if they will let me go. The captors keep asking how much money we have in our accounts and seem dissatisfied with the amount. They shake their heads in disagreement and talk among themselves in their native language. They are after fast cash and a lot of it, too. For a moment, they seem to be considering Brendan's offer. Brendan thinks of methods to get us out of this situation. He considers overpowering the one, grabbing his hand holding the firearm and using it to shoot the other captor. Brendan is not an aggressive person, so this type of act does not come naturally to him. He pauses to think it through.

From the conversations, we can now pick up that they have already planned to dispose of us once they have what they need.

The phone rings. The withdrawal is complete.

"It's time," the one says. "Get up!"

We are taken further into the veld. They seem to know where they are going. It's is like they had planned it all carefully, before they took us hostage. They are noticeably more aggressive towards us. I can hear the sound of a gun cocking coming from behind me.

What did they mean by, "It is time?"

I have prepared myself for death. A strange calmness has come over me and I am no longer afraid of dying. I think about my parents one more time. I hope that they will be able to accept the news. I have been praying the whole night and I have given everything over to God now.

"This is it, this is the spot," the slightly more composed man says.

On the way there, Brendan had told me to run when he gave the signal. He would distract them long enough for me to get away. We have reached a large tree that grows on the edge of a deep ditch. *It would take someone a long time to find us here. We'll be missing for quite some time before anyone realises that something must have happened to us.*

Brendan and I have been separated and the profligate thug, who has been harassing me all along, seems pleased to have me for himself and under his control. "Where is the sex?" he asks.

I am willing to die, but I am not going to live through this first.

"I'll kill you with my bare hands before I let you touch me!" I shout in defiance.

"Do you know what this is?" he asks, while aggressively pointing the gun at me.

"Yes, and I'm not afraid of you!"

"You are not afraid of this?" With that, he hits me on my jaw, using the edge of his firearm. I feel dizzy for a few seconds. Complete blackness overcomes me, but I force myself to stay strong and manage to shake the feeling. I find enough strength inside myself to shove the robust, diabolic man so that he stumbles a few steps backwards. Brendan is tussling with another man and shouts for me to run. I hesitate for a moment. The two robbers are shouting something to each other, again in their own language. They are both focused on Brendan for a moment, nervous that he may get away, which gives me a gap to escape.

It's a very dark night; there is almost no moon. I can hardly see more than a metre ahead of me. I keep stumbling on the uneven earth. There are holes and wires everywhere. I fall with every few steps. In a panic, I call out to Brendan. I feel lost in the darkness. I am out of breath and my legs are burning from the razor-wire cuts. I keep running, without any idea of where I am going. I know that there is a squatter camp somewhere close-by; I can smell the fires and an aroma of cooking pap hangs in the cold air. I am terrified to end up there. It is no place for a young, white girl. There may be someone there who could help me, but I may also run into the wrong people. I have no idea where Brendan is. I don't know if the men have caught up with him; that is my worst fear. Again, I call out to him in the blackness of the night, desperate to get a response. I would do anything to see him again. The attempt to find him drains my last bit of energy. I collapse onto the ground, feeling sorry for myself. *Get up, you must keep going. There is no time for tears now. Pull yourself together.* I pep-talk myself to find my last bit of strength.

After what feels like miles of pitch darkness, I finally reach a wire fence, where I can see a light on inside the small cottage-style house, surrounded by a large area of farmland. Relieved, I start calling out for help. There are two large-breed dogs - Boerboels or mastiffs, with lion-sized heads - on the property, barking in deep snarls of warning.

"Help, help," I weep in desperation. I have my fingers hooked through the wire like a desperate prisoner, exhausted and struggling to get the words out. I know that the barking will eventually alert the people inside the house. An old man comes out, with a big, blindingly-bright flashlight. He is dumbstruck to find me standing there, like Snow White who escaped the huntsman and ran from the woods. I am a complete mess. My clothes are torn and dirty and I'm covered in blood, from stumbling over pieces of razor-wire. The old man explains to me to go around the fence to his gate, which is on the other side of the property. As the gate opens, the dogs run straight for me, still barking and upset by the unknown intruder. I don't give them a second thought, my relief at finding someone to help is far too great.

I am invited inside. It's an old farmhouse, but it is neat and homely. The old man introduces himself as John. The furniture in the house reminds me of my grandmother's house; she passed away in September of the previous year.

"Come, sit down," John says. He has a gentle face, with soft lines around his pale grey eyes. "You have to help Brendan," I plead. "I can't sit, we have to find him. Can you take me back?" I ask, while aimlessly walking up and down looking out the windows of the quaint house.

"Let call the cops," John responds. I nod in agreement. His wife had been asleep, but has been woken by the commotion. She switches on the kettle to make us a cup of tea.

"Sit down, honey," she says, while comforting me. The couch is covered with a throw-over blanket to hide the wear-and-tear that comes from years of use. There is crocheted cloth protecting the old, wooden, antique coffee table. John puts an ashtray down on the table and offers me a cigarette.

"No, thank you, Sir"

"Margaret is bringing your tea."

I am too emotional to answer and nod my head in appreciation. The old man spends over fifteen minutes on the phone, trying to explain to the police what has happened and where to find us.
He gets annoyed when he realises that they will not be of much help to us. I get more and more anxious and beg him again to help me find Brendan. John tells me to wait with his wife and leaves in his white Toyota 4x4 bakkie to see if he can find any trace of Brendan.

Brendan had run in a different direction and had reached a few farms on the other side. He had jumped over electric fences and knocked on doors and windows to find help. He had no idea what had happened to me, either, and was looking for someone to help, especially with a weapon, to find me. Nobody would open their doors for him. It was understandable; everyone has the same fears. We have all stopped trusting one another. One of the guys he met had called out his armed-response security company to assist. Meanwhile, Brendan had armed himself with a large stick and had gone back to where he'd last seen me. On the way, he'd met up with the security-guard, who had arrived within a few minutes after being called. The two of them had started searching the area. John arrives a few minutes later. He can see the search lights and emergency lights from the security vehicle.

"Brendan, Brendan!" he calls out. Brendan looks over to John, squinting his eyes to try and see him better. All the lights are blinding. "Danelle is over at my house!"

Brendan gets into the bakkie with John. "Please take me to her," he responds gratefully.

I have been looking out for the lights of John's bakkie returning home. I pray that Brendan is with John. As the lights approach, I run to the porch and wait anxiously on the step by the front door.
The bakkie stops and both men get out.

"There is a God," Brendan says in disbelief to see me alive. His places his hands firmly on my shoulders and stares at me for a little while longer. I can't get out a single word, but just start sobbing. I cry for the first time since the whole ordeal started. Brendan pulls me close to his chest and hugs me tightly. "You are very strong," he says, while softly caressing my face.

The cops arrive about five minutes later. It's difficult to give a statement. It's hard to relive the whole ordeal so soon after it's just happened. The policemen make me uncomfortable. I keep looking down at their firearms. They ask me the same questions over and over, as if they do not understand my description of the events. I feel like one of their suspects. They are rude and unhelpful.
I get emotional and start shaking.

"We'll give our statements to the detectives in the morning," Brendan says, noticing that I am not in any state to talk to them right now. John drives us back to where we were parked.

CHAPTER 7

Brendan spends what is left of the night with me at Kim and Alsten's house. We get cleaned up in the shower and then get straight into bed, but neither of us can fall asleep. The scenario runs through my head. The happenings repeat, over and over and over. *Sometimes I wish that I could turn my thoughts off, clear my mind completely.*

I keep looking over at my watch for the time. I remember that one of the attackers grabbed my wrist and looked at my watch, while we'd been held captive in the veld. He'd decided not to take it. He probably didn't think it was worth anything. It is a DKNY watch I got for Christmas from my parents. It has a small, square face, in a larger mat-silver frame and a broad black leather strap. I am happy that he didn't take it. It is of sentimental value to me. My rings and silver necklace were taken, however. I know that Brendan will tease me about the fact that the robber wasn't interested in taking my watch. Brendan has never liked it. I anxiously wait for the time to pass so that I can get up and go to work. I need the distraction. At 5am, I get back into the shower. The warm water running down my back seems to calm me. The cuts on my legs are stinging.

Today, after the horror, the world seems different. People look different. The near-death experience has brought on a sense of newness to the world around me. As I drive through the traffic and look at other people in their cars, I wonder what they are feeling today, what they are possibly dealing with and if they are viewing things around them the same way that I am. I watch all their different expressions. Some are aggressive; some are annoyed by the traffic and others seem anxious about being late for an important meeting, perhaps. Someone smiles at me and I realise that I am staring. I quickly look away and turn up the radio. Somehow, the warm smile from a stranger gives comfort. I am surprised by it.

I arrive at work and try to keep myself composed. I knew that Liezille will pick up immediately that something is wrong, so I try to slip past her as quickly as possible, as I go up the stairs and into my office. *I am not ready to talk about it. I do not want to get emotional and weak at work.* I sit down in my office chair in a kind of a trance. The phone rings, it is an internal call. I can tell by the type of ring. It's Liezille. "What is up with you today? Come on, out with it, how was your weekend? Is Brendan back yet? I am making coffee; I'll be in your office in 5."

Liezille and I have become very close over the months that we have worked together. We are in a small office building, which has only seven offices. It's an informal work environment. When I am not busy at my desk, I often go down to her office and have coffee. I get lonely in my office, which is upstairs, next to that of the Chief Executive Officer's and the Chief Financial Officer's office. They travel most of the time and I have the whole floor to myself. The ladies downstairs all share the same office and there are three other offices on the lower level. It is always buzzing with conversation there. The office walls used to be white, but I convinced my boss to give me a budget to add some colour to the place. I added a few feminine touches to give it some life. The walls were painted with a warmer tone and carpets were installed in each office. I appreciate beautiful surroundings; it is something that is very important to me. I am highly affected by my environment.

Liezille slowly puts down the two mugs of coffee, while staring at me like I am a stranger. She can tell by my blank expression and the empty look in my eyes that there is something serious that I'm about to tell her.

"Danellie, what is it? Talk to me".

I fight back the tears. "We were kidnapped last night. Err…I mean, abducted, I think that is the right term". I take a deep breath, then a sip of coffee. My hands are shaking and I must concentrate not to spill. I slowly place the cup back on my desk. I proceed to tell Liezille the whole story.

"What are you doing here? You are a wreck. You

need to go home and deal with this."

"I don't know where to go. I feel a bit like a fish out of water."

"Why don't you go to your parents?"

My parents! It suddenly dawns on me: *They are still completely oblivious to what happened to me last night.* With all that has been going on, I haven't managed to find a moment to contact them. *I don't want to burden them with this, but I don't want them to hear it from someone else, either.* I dial their home number. I have to redial the numbers a few times. The number sequence of their home phone, that is usually second nature for my figures on the keypad, is suddenly a blank space in my head. My mom answers. For the first few moments after she picks up the phone I am completely silent. Speechless. Where do I start?

"Hello, hello…"

"Mom, Mom, it's me. I'm just phoning to let you know that you won't be able to get hold of me on my phone. It was stolen last night." That's all I can get out, before I get an uncomfortable feeling in my throat from swallowing the emotion.

How do I put this in words? I give my mom the short version. I tell her the important parts. The most important part is that I'm alive and unharmed. But I am still in shock. Liezille has left to go and speak to my boss. My office phone rings. It's him on the line. "I want you to go home. Take as much time as you need. Come back when you are ready."

I feel lost. I want to be alone. I want to hide away from everything and everyone. I want to crawl under the blankets on my bed and pretend that it was all a bad dream. I want to cry where no one can see me. *But I don't want to be alone either, I am afraid to be by myself.*

I don't remember feeling this bad when we were armed robbery in April of 1992. I suppose that it was different then. I was only nine, a young and innocent child. I didn't completely realise the dangers then. Death and rape are not things a kid understands. I didn't truly believe then that someone would kill another for no reason at all. Last night, I prepared myself to leave this earth. I prepared myself to die unnecessarily by the hands of thugs. The hatred in their eyes was disturbing. *How do you hate someone you do not know?* So many thoughts crossed my mind. I thought back on my life. On the choices I had made. I thought about the people in my life and how they would react when I am gone. I thought about what I would be missing out on – marriage, kids of my own.

I would never look at life and people the same way again. I would never forget how much I really love Brendan. I would never stop appreciating him.

CHAPTER 8

The months following the attack were emotionally exhausting. At times I could talk about what had happened, as if completely disconnected from it. It was as if I was telling someone about a movie I had seen, a fiction. I could relay my story without any feeling, completely and utterly emotionally numb. I must have told the story a hundred times over. I would have to tell it to another friend joining in a conversation, to another family member or relative. Somehow, the subject kept coming up. The more I told the story, the more distant it became to me; the more I could separate myself from it, the less I felt.

Then there were the flashbacks. Involuntary thought and feelings would take over my mind. Vivid memories of the event would come back to haunt me at times. I remember driving in the car once, on the same road where the abduction had happened. Brendan and I were going out for dinner and a movie, when I'd suddenly felt overwhelmed with fear. The people walking on the streets had suddenly turned into monsters. I'd watched as their faces had physically changed into evil devilish beings. I'd felt them all staring at me, like predators pursuing prey. The vulnerability I'd felt was unbearable. *It was a scene out of Zombieland - the aimless wanderings of seemingly soulless people.* I could feel my heartbeat increasing, my palms getting sweaty, and I felt light-headed. I had to force the images from my thoughts.

"What happened?" Brendan had asked, concerned.

I'd been unable to explain myself. "Nothing. They just scare me. The people on the streets. I was reminded of that night."

What unsettled me most in the succeeding days was the loss of power I had felt during the attack. They had robbed me of my free will to decide over my own life. For those few hours, they had dictated my life. Life and death had been out of my control; it had been governed by cruel criminals. I had felt weak. Helpless.

That's it, I think after another episode of panic, I refuse to let them have any more control over my life. *I am ultimately the master of my own mind. I have control over my cognitive processes - to a certain extent, at least. Mind over matter.*

While captive at gunpoint, my mind had often wondered. I had withdrawn into myself, as I always do when I am placed under stress. The commands and threats of the robbers had become background noise.

What has happened in their lives to make them do this? I believe that everything can be understood by means of cause and effect. *They were not born evil, were they? Once upon a time, they were innocent babies cuddled in the loving arms of their mothers. Innocent and impressionable babies. Where did things go wrong for them?* For a few moments, I had felt empathy towards the attackers. They were human after all, and not the beasts that they were portraying themselves to be.

Our socio-economic situation is probably largely to blame for the bad things that people do. The truth is that many African children grow up without parents. HIV and AIDS (acquired immune deficiency syndrome) is largely to blame for this. They have to face the world on their own, without love and support. Without guidance or direction, they do what they have to, to survive. Mother Theresa once said that,

"There is more hunger for love and appreciation in this world than for bread". I tend to agree.

By the end of January 2007, I was enrolled as a student at the University of South Africa for a degree in Applied Psychology. I took modules dealing with Language, Attitude and World View, Basic Psychology and Psychology in Society. I didn't go and see a psychologist after the ordeal; I would empower myself, instead. I have always been a keen observer of human behaviour and was excited to expand on my knowledge on the topic. I am naturally perceptive and aware of people's body language; I have a sixth sense for that kind of thing. I often boast about the fact that I can read someone within a few minutes of meeting them. *And I am hardly ever wrong.* Through expressions, gapes and gestures, people reveal secrets about themselves. It is an unspoken language we all use, one that always reveals the truth. I am fascinated by the subject. More than anything, I had hoped to gain insight about myself, my own mental state and that of my attackers as well.

Studying created a great distraction, the kind of distraction I needed. I had less time to think about what had happened and how it had made me feel. My mind became occupied with theories - theories about human behaviour, about perceptions and about culture. I had been warned not to fall into the trap of "I have it, too," or "medical student syndrome". It is apparently common for medical or psychology students to look at the symptoms of a disorder and recognise it as their own, or ascribe it to people they know, like family and friends. The truth is that many of the indicators described as mental disorders are common traits found in all of us. Take, for example, the description of Narcissistic Personality Disorder. People suffering from this disorder are described as people with an exaggerated sense of self-importance; they seek attention and admiration, and talk mainly about themselves in conversations with others. They have a sense of entitlement, self-importance and idealise unlimited success, and so on and so on. I know many people with these characteristics. In fact, most people I know behave like this most of the time. You just have to look at social media these days and you could probably describe most of today's population as a bunch of narcissists. The more I learnt about the different personality disorders, the more I understood the reason for this important paragraph and warning in the prologue of my text books. I came to believe that I knew antisocial, schizophrenic and psychopathic people. And, by then, I was convinced that I was suffering from Post-traumatic Stress Disorder. I decided to steer clear of self-diagnosis and, instead, kept my focus removed from my own problems. I felt drawn to a collection of scientific studies by the great forefathers of psychology.

In the February of that year, Brendan and I decided to take a short holiday. My parents had a holiday house in Umhlanga Rocks, North of Durban, that they made available to us. It was a beautiful house, within walking distance of the beach, with a large garden and a pool. I spent a great deal of my childhood in this house. I always loved the time there and, when I grew up, I always remembered it as a place far away from my troubles. The distance from the house in Johannesburg to the house in Umhlanga felt like an escape; for that short period of time, I could leave the other 'life' behind. There were no bad memories in that house, only pleasant ones of warm summer days and

Christmas dinners. The sea had always been a calming refuge for my soul. The house had a separate flatlet attached to it that Uncle Kim and Aunt Maria rented from my parents. They weren't relatives to me, but I had known them since the age of six, and referred to them as Uncle and Aunt out of respect. They were, in many ways, like grandparents to me. On this trip, I was eager to introduce Brendan to them. Uncle Kim and Aunt Maria both passed away within the year to follow, mere months apart of each other.

Brendan had to work on Valentine's Day, so we had postponed the whole romantic celebration for a week. Brendan is not one for these things, but I had insisted that any excuse to do something special, something other than the normal, was good enough reason to commemorate the day. I feel the same about Christmas and birthday celebrations. I made my point by purchasing a sultry red dress and lingerie to match, coupled with a pair of chic, stylish black heels that showed off my pedicured toenails. This way I got him enthusiastic about it, too. I was excited to spend some quality time together. Most of the tension of an ordeal still fresh in my memory, was lifted when we reached the coastline and the salty air entered my senses. We picked a quiet little restaurant on the beach for dinner.

In conversation, at a table that overlooked the calming sea, and with the hot, summer air blowing in a soft breeze, we went back to that January night. It's like a

healing wound you are still reminded of by a discomforting itch. It is an experience not easily forgotten.
The talk about it was much lighter now that we had had some time to process it. This time, we downplayed the events. "Robbers should consider setting themselves up with card facilities. I mean, who still carries cash in the 21st century?"

With mood-lightening repartee, Brendan and I joked about it. "I don't have cash, do you take plastic?" We both chuckle at the strange concept.

It was refreshing to be able to laugh about it for a change. Many things are cured with humour I believe, even dark humour. But, behind the casual remarks, we were still masking a serious matter. The trauma had left scars, and although we have healed slowly over time, we will never be completely unaffected.

People often remarked how lucky we were. Lucky, we were not killed. Lucky, we were not seriously harmed and lucky I was never raped. I never *felt* lucky when they said these things to me. Their callous remarks even annoyed me. It was not until years later, when I listened to the story of another young girl who had not been as lucky, that I realised what they had meant.

CHAPTER 9

It is March of 2007 and we have just found out that we are expecting a baby. Liezille recommends her gynaecologist to me. He is based at a private hospital in Bedfordview, approximately 15 minutes from the office. I decide to suppress any emotions about the pregnancy until it is confirmed by a doctor. I am not ready to accept that my whole life is about to change by believing two lines on a pee stick. I am well aware how the science of it all works and that the test can detect the presence of hCG, a human growth hormone that is only produced by the body when a woman is pregnant. I have googled it a thousand times, but I still want the doctor to confirm the existence of a baby.

I am very nervous about my appointment. It is the very first time ever that I am going to see a gynaecologist. I know women are supposed to visit a gyno often to make sure there are no health issues, but I cannot help but be uncomfortable with the idea. Until now, I have never had a real reason to make an appointment. I ask Liezille to go with me on the first visit. *If the doctor confirms the pregnancy, Brendan can accompany me for all the visits to follow.*

We sit in the waiting-room for about 45 minutes, before the doc can see me.

"I'm not sure if I'm ready for this. I don't know if I am ready to hear what he is about to tell me," I say to Liezille, while trying to get comfortable in the chair.

"You'll be fine," Liezille responds, with her usual warm smile.

I get up to pour myself a glass of water and offer some to Liezille too. Liezille and Drikus have been trying to conceive for a while now. It has been months. I know how badly she wants to be a mommy. *Isn't life strange? Liezille is hoping with all her heart to fall pregnant, but instead I'm pregnant. I'm pregnant and completely unprepared.*

"Soon it will be your turn, I know it. You'll soon be waiting in this very room for the doctor to see you," I say to her, feeling slightly guilty about my latest stroke of good luck.

My name is being called. The doctor comes out and greets me in the waiting-room. He is a tall man, with a warm smile. His hands are pale and soft.

"Please come through." He directs me to a chair at his desk. I carefully pull out the chair and sit down. I can be very clumsy at times, especially when I feel stressed. The doctor briefly introduces himself as Doctor Van den Bergh and then looks down at my file to read the information I have provided. I was handed forms to complete upon arrival.

"Miss Dames, can I call you Danelle? I have to ask you a few personal questions, if you don't mind. It is important for me to know your health background. If you are indeed expecting, we want to give this baby the best chance of a healthy pregnancy and birth. If there are any potential complications or things we need to be concerned about, we need to make provision for it."

I nod in agreement. Both my hands are tightly gripping onto my thighs, slightly above each knee. I try to conceal the tension, but I'm sure it is easily noticeable that I am feeling a bit uneasy. Fortunately, I am not the first woman the doc has met who is anxious about an unexpected expectancy.

The doctor proceeds to ask me about my family's health history, as well as any health issues that have affected my life. "Forgive me for asking this, but it is part of the normal questions I ask all my patients. How many sexual partners do you have?"

"One, only one. I'm in a monogamous relationship. There has been no one else." I answer quickly and seriously. I don't want the doctor to get the wrong impression about me, just because I'm unmarried.

"Good," the doctor responds slightly amused, "then we don't have to worry about a paternity test."

The doctor explains that he will require a blood test and also will have to do tests for a variety of things, including sexually- transmitted diseases and to ascertain my blood type. He asks my permission to test for HIV and Aids. Next the gyno points me to the examination room and explains that I should get undressed and put on the robe that is provided. I am asked to take off everything else.

"On the shelf, you will see a glass that almost looks like a Champagne glass. It is not for celebrating, that comes later. We'll need a urine sample to test for urinary-tract infections. After that, you can weigh yourself on the scale by the door. Don't worry, we'll keep that number a secret. You only have to tell me."

I appreciate his sense of humour. After a full head-to-toe examination, I am asked to put my clothes back on and to return for the ultrasound.
That wasn't half as bad as I'd expected it to be.

"Would your mom like to join us for this?" the doctor asks, referring to Liezille.

"Oh, she's not my mother," I respond laughingly. "If she was, she would have been nine when she had me."

People often perceive me as younger than my actual age.

Usually I don't mind that I look younger than I am. But when you are pregnant, the last thing you want is for everyone to think that you are just another case of a teen pregnancy. People also don't take you seriously when they think of you as a youngster, especially in business. I'm still asked to present my ID whenever I enter a bar or a club with any of my friends. I suppose that doesn't matter now. *Those days are in the past. Instead, I'll be home looking after a baby, feeding and changing nappies.*

Suddenly I feel uneasy again. The doctor squirts cold jelly onto my tummy and starts with the ultrasound. For a few minutes, there is absolute silence in the room while the doctor moves the ultrasound probe from side to side and in slow upand-down motions over my abdomen. Then he presses down on a spot, while checking the ultrasound screen. He moves it slightly and applies pressure once more. "Congratulations! There's your little baby. About the size of a kidney bean now." He fiddles with something on his equipment. "Let's see if we can pick up the heartbeat, shall we?"
And there it is - a little heart is beating inside my belly. A new life is growing inside of me. No-one or nothing can ever prepare you for this moment in time. The

moment when you realise that you are going to be a parent. From this day onwards, I am responsible for another life. Life is not just about me anymore; I have a new purpose. The whole appointment is over in about 35 minutes. I leave with a prescription for prenatal vitamins.

I start dialling Brendan's number as I leave the doctors rooms. "It official, we are going to be parents!"

I am overwhelmed with emotion. It feels like I am experiencing about a hundred different conflicting emotions, all at the same time. I feel excited but scared, blessed but surprised, overjoyed but unsure, amazed but terrified. *To think, only a few months ago I believed that Brendan and I were both going to die. Instead, we have created a new life, conceived a new being. A little person is growing inside of me with each new day. He is half-me and half-Brendan.*

CHAPTER 10

My parents were, at first, disconcerted about the announcement of my pregnancy. They are conservative when it comes to things like this. First comes love, then comes marriage and only then comes a baby. I was terrified to tell them. I couldn't find the words. I decided to tell my sister first. I knew that she would find it impossible to keep a secret and I used that as an ice-breaker.

After taking time to process it, the news was received with loving wishes. My dad greeted me with a big hug. "Congratulations to you both," he said, while holding me in a firm embrace. My mom went out and bought the baby his first outfit. It was neatly placed on the bed in the room I used to sleep in.

I am conservative in love, too, but for me, marriage does not necessarily equate with love. Love and commitment can exist without marriage. It is ultimately nothing more than a piece of paper binding two people by law. A committed and loving relationship between two people carries far more weight than a certificate of marriage. Don't get me wrong, it's not that I don't believe in the institution of marriage; it's just that I don't believe it is substantial validation for either the presence or absence of love. In history, marriage was established for the purpose of forming a strategic alliance between two families. It is only much later that the meaning of marriage changed to the happily-ever-after that we believe it to be.

I have this argument with my brother-in-law, Andries, during my pregnancy. Andries and Dornè are married and have a baby boy named Barnard. Barnard was born on the 30th of April. She was still pregnant with him when I found out that I was also expecting. Andries, in all his wisdom, decided to argue the topic of having a baby out of wedlock, over dinner one night with my parents. Andries is one of those "know it all" people. He is very opinionated. He argues for the sake of arguing. "I don't want my son to be exposed to this child when they grow up," he says in conversation. "It will teach him immorality. Children should be born to married parents. That is what the Bible teaches us and it is what society expects from us."

"What about divorced parents? "I argued. "How do you feel about that then? Does the Bible not say that it is also a sin to get divorced, yet your parents are divorced? Heck, my dad got divorced from his first wife, too. Have you ever thought about the fact that words carry different meanings at different stages of time? That the original meaning of something is not necessarily the same meaning that we assign to it now? Who knows what the meaning of marriage was in biblical times. Marriage is something we invented. It is manmade, not godly."

My sister supported him in this feud. She has, over the years of being with him, lost the ability to make up her own mind about things. She has learned to adopt his opinion on issues and lost herself in the process.

"It is unacceptable in our society, no matter how you try and argue it. A bastard child is still a bastard child," he carries on.

I want to ask him about same-sex marriages, like the one his dad is in. And that I am convinced that he is gay, too. *I have no problem with homosexuality, some of my best friends are gay, but if he wants to argue things based on the Bible, there should be no exclusions to suit him.* I want
to tell him that he is a hypocrite. But I don't. Instead, I walk away. *I am not even sure why I am so upset; some fights are not worth the energy you waste on them.* But I am distraught. I'm upset that my sister didn't stand up for me but, instead, supported his notion. She used to protect my honour against everyone. We used to look out for each other. *Would she genuinely keep her child away from his cousin only because Brendan and I are not married?*

After that, I decided to distance myself from everybody and everything that left me feeling hurt. I had enough to think about, without adding other peoples' negative comments into the mix. There was no greater judge of me than I was of myself. I had never been harder on myself than I was right then, at that stage in my life.

I can forgive myself for failing at many things, but I'll not allow myself to fail as a mother.

The responsibility of becoming a mom rested heavily on my shoulders. *Will I be a good mother? Will I know how to teach someone the difference between right and wrong? What if I can't protect him or her against the evils of the world?*

For the most part, I had an uncomplicated and healthy pregnancy. I didn't experience any of the discomforts that most women describe. My sister suffered severe nausea during her first trimester with Barnard. She experienced fatigue, swelling in her legs, skin changes, heartburn and indigestion. She said that she had been uncomfortable from the day she first realised that she was pregnant, until the day Barnard was born.

I enjoyed being pregnant. I had never loved my body more. I religiously took my vitamins every morning after breakfast, a habit I had to force myself to adopt. I had never been good with taking medication regularly, but the importance of folic acid for the baby's development had been clearly explained to me by the doctor. This time around, it was not only my health that could be affected, but I was now responsible for another innocent life. I cut out coffee and only drank

Rooibos tea, the only tea that contains no caffeine. I avoided foods like sushi – and boy do I love raw salmon! – and cold meats that could potentially be harmful to the foetus. I ordered mineral water instead of soft drinks, whenever we went out to a restaurant. I maintained a healthy fitness level and body weight. My focus was 100% on the health of our unborn child. I wanted to give him the best chance in life, starting from even before he was born.

On 29 September 2007, I go out shopping for the last baby necessities still left on my list. Brendan left early in the morning for a work project in the Free State. He has been taking on a few new business ventures to supplement our income. I have noticed that he has been a bit tense for a while now. He rarely discusses his feelings with me, but I know that the pressure of becoming a dad again is getting to him. He is worried about failing to provide for us. He still feels guilty about not having been able to protect me on the night of the attack and now he is worried about how he will protect a baby. He has always felt as if he let his other kids down, one way or another; even though he only has the best intentions to be a good father to them. And he is worried that history will repeat itself.
I try not to place any additional pressure on him. I allow him to work through this on his own. He will come around. He is a good father to his other kids and I know he will be a good father to our son, too. I know his heart better than anyone else does. He will be back

from his trip early Monday morning. I spend most of Saturday morning shopping for baby items. My due date is the 12th of November, but I like to have everything prepared before then, to calm my nerves. I changed my gynaecologist to the doctor who brought my sister's son, Barnard, into the world. My sister insisted that I set up an appointment with her. Dr. Brink is a female doctor, with a practice at the new private hospital in Fourways. Brendan and I are renting a small cottage in Chartwell, a farmland area in the North of Johannesburg. Our home is exactly five minutes away from the hospital, so it made sense for me to change doctors. Dr. Van den Bergh's practice is based in the Bedfordview Private Hospital, which is close the office, but about 75km away from home. I doubt that I'll still be at work when the time comes for the baby to be born. My maternity leave is already booked for 2 weeks before my due date. Dr. Brink is highly-respected in the field of gynaecology and obstetrics, so I feel comfortable that she will be my doctor during labour.

I get home and make myself a cup of tea. I make sure that all the doors, and the security-gate at the front door, are locked. Excitedly, I go through all the packets I've bought, imagining what it will feel like to hold my little boy in my arms. I take the tiny clothes to the washing-machine and add a cup of extra-sensitive washing-detergent to the load. All the baby clothes are washed before they are packed away in the chest of drawers, a gift I received from everyone at work. My mom phones just as I finish my dinner, to check how I'm feeling.

"Are your bags packed and ready for the hospital?" she asks.

"Mom, I'm still a little over 6 weeks away from my due date. That would be a bit over-eager, don't you think?"

"It's best to be prepared, Danelle; you never know what can happen." *It reminds me of the speech she used to give me about wearing decent underwear. "You never know when you could be in a car accident,"* she used to preach.

"Yes, Mom, I'm sure it won't hurt to get it ready." I open the large suitcase on the bed and start packing. The hospital has given me a long list of things to take with me. I feel exhausted afterwards and fall asleep to *The Notebook*, one of my favourite romantic movies. At 10pm, I wake up in terrible pain. I toss and turn, trying to get comfortable, desperate to get back to sleep. I've read about Braxton Hicks, named after an English doctor back in 1872. He explained that midpregnancy pains were just 'contractions preparing you for labour'. *That is probably all it is.* The last bit of *The Notebook* is still on; I try to watch it, to force my attention away from the pain. The next contraction is even more intense than the one before.

I've heard that a warm bath will stop Braxton Hicks, so this is what I'll do. Exhausted and weak, I get out of bed and walk over to the bathroom to run the bathwater. As I reach the bathroom, I have another painful contraction. Unable to stand, I hunch over the bath and grip onto the rim for support. When that one is over, I get into the bath, but the water barely covers the bottom of the bath. It's an old farmhouse, with a steel bath and low water-pressure. I'm extremely uncomfortable.

The bath is cold and hard and I am in a lot of pain. I wish I can make the water run faster. I decide to get out and back into bed, but I'm uncomfortable no matter what I try. I get back into the bath. My body feels like it has been taken over by some unnatural force. Like an alien scene from the movies, when they procure human bodies. My belly is moving and pulling into an odd oblong shape, with a defined point.

I must get to a hospital. If this baby wants to be born, I am not having it here. I am not giving birth by myself. Terrified, I start sobbing. I hardly have the strength to lift myself out of the bath. I wobble over to the bedroom and sit down on the bed to compose myself, before I find the strength to get dressed. I look over at the suitcase. *How did she know?* I am too weak to lift the suitcase. It will have to wait.

I unlock the door and security-gate. Then sit down as another contraction takes over. *I won't be able to drive in this condition.* I look at my watch to see how far apart the contractions are. I get into my car and wait for another contraction to be over. That will give me an eight-minute interlude to get to the hospital before I have another one. The hospital is about five minutes away.

I don't make it inside to the reception area of the hospital. Instead I collapse, with another painful tightening sensation in my abdomen. I am kneeling on the ground, with my hands flat on the tar in the parking lot a few metres in front of the entrance doors, when the security-guard comes running towards me. Still wary after the attack on us by a guy dressed in a security uniform, I apprehensively indicate to him that I am fine by raising my left hand. I hastily get back up onto my feet and proceed to Reception.

The receptionist barely looks up at me.

"Excuse me, ma'am, are you able to help me? I think I may be in labour. Premature labour. My due date is not until 6 weeks from now," I say desperately.

"The maternity ward is that way," she says, pointing down the passage to the left. I am too uncomfortable to walk properly. I'm holding on firmly, supporting the bottom of my belly as though to stop the baby from falling out.

I seem to go unnoticed in the maternity ward. "Excuse me, please help me," I plead with a nurse passing by.

"Yes, my dear, what seems to be the problem?"

"I think I may be in labour, but I'm not due yet! You must stop it! Please, you have to stop the contractions!"

The nurse looks at me, incredulous. "How did you get here, dear?"

"I drove myself. I timed my contractions and managed to make it here in between the cramps."

"How far along are you?" she wants to know.

"It is all in my file. I was here to book my hospital bed just last week. I'm supposed to see Dr. Brink again on Tuesday. I'll be 34 weeks then."

"Let's get you into bed."

The nurse takes my blood pressure. She gently helps me up to a sitting position and wraps a belt, connected to a tocodynamometer, around my waste to monitor the contractions. The tears are streaming down my face. I am surrounded by people yet have never felt so lonely.

"You can lie down now, dear." The needle of the tocodynamometer is moving up and down, showing high peaks on a graph sheet. "I'll call the doctor. He'll be here soon to come and see to you. Try to relax now; it is not good for the baby if you are stressed," the nurse says while she puts a drip in my arm and then leaves the room.

I am somewhat in a daze by the time the doctor comes to see me. He walks in and, without any introduction, picks up my file to study it. He proceeds to do a pelvic examination. He picks up my file again to make a note. He is about to walk off when I call him back. "Doctor, can you please tell me what is going on? Is the baby okay?" I ask in a panic.

"You are in labour," he responds. "You are about 5cm dilated."

"No!" I cry, almost hysterical. "It's too soon!" "The baby is coming today, whether you like it or not. There is nothing we can do to stop it now," the doctor arrogantly replies. "The nurse will prepare you for theatre, for an emergency Csection."

I'm not comfortable with this doctor. He gives me the creeps. He is rude and arrogant.

"Nurse, please get hold of Dr. Brink. Please make sure that she is the one who will be operating on me. I'm still trying to get hold of Brendan, the father. Please tell them to wait till I do. Until I can speak to him. Please." This is not at all the way I imagined this day. A girl dreams of two days in her life. Her wedding day and the day she has her first child. This is not the special day I'd been hoping for. I try Brendan's phone again, but it is still off. It is 2am in the morning. He is probably fast asleep, completely oblivious to what I am going through. The nurse comes back with news from Dr. Brink. "She asked for a report. It looks like she will postpone the operation until 8am. That is the very latest. She said that she will be in shortly to check on you herself. Is there someone else I can phone for you, dear?

"I can't phone my parents at this hour. They will go into a complete panic. My dad is too old to deal with this kind of stress. Kim, I'll phone Kim. Sweet and reliable Kim. Kim and Alsten arrive at the hospital 45 minutes later. I have no idea how they made it here in such a short time. "Kimmie." That's all I can get out before I start sobbing.

"It's okay, everything will be okay. What do you need? Can I get you something?"

"My bag, I left it at the house."

"Is it packed? Alsten will go and fetch it. I'll stay here with you."

At 6am, I ask Kim to contact my parents. "Please tell them not to rush. I'm only going in at eight." I try Brendan's phone once more, but still to no avail. I think I saw his charger at home when I packed my bag. His phone battery is probably flat.
I'll have to accept that I'm doing this without him. Even if I do get hold of him now, he will never make it here in time.

My parents arrive while the anaesthetist completes his examination. He checks my blood pressure and takes a detailed health history. "Will someone be going with you into theatre?" the nurse asks.

"Yes, my mother," I respond quickly. I'm not giving her any time to back out. I know she is very squeamish, but I need her in there with me.

"Then come with me, please ma'am, we need to get you ready."

My mom returns, wearing a long green gown, a protective cap covering her hair, and covers over her shoes. As soon as she gets back, I am wheeled off to the theatre. It's a few minutes before 8am.

The operating-room is cold, with big, bright lights. There are a few people inside, waiting for me. I am moved from the bed onto the operating-table. Next to the table is a stainless-steel tray with instruments. I can feel the anxiety building up inside of me; it is a paralysing feeling. I recognise the anaesthetist. The nurse gave me a tablet to take on the way into theatre to "take the edge off" as she put it, but it is not doing anything for me yet.

"It's a bit late, but it should still help to calm you," she'd said.

A pulse-oximeter machine is attached to my index finger. Before long, I feel drowsy and tired. My limbs feel heavy and I am slightly disoriented and confused. I'm not sure if this is caused by the anxiety or by the anaesthetic. There are about ten people in the room with me now, including Dr. Brink. They are having a casual conversation, while preparing for the C-section. The anaesthetist constantly checks with me that I am still responsive and gets worried when I don't answer. I'm in a complete daze. I look up at my mom.

"Almost there," Mom says to comfort me.

Within minutes, Spencer is born. The doctor brings him over for a few seconds and then he is rushed away to neonatal ICU.

"Her blood pressure is falling!" the doctor says in a panic. I wake up hours later in my hospital room.

"Push this button if you are in pain, dear," the nurse explains. "It's a morphine drip."

All I want is to see my baby boy.

Spencer is connected to machines to help him breathe. His lungs are still undeveloped; they must develop outside of the womb now. The paediatrician, Dr. Ahmed, explains that they have given Spencer steroids to speed up the lungdevelopment process. The next few hours are critical and there is a high risk that he will not pull through. He has a feeding-tube that runs from his nose all the way down into his tiny tummy. He is too small to suck. The ability for a baby to suck only develops in the later weeks of pregnancy.
Spencer is 6 weeks and 3 days premature.

Brendan arrives a few hours later. He finally got all my messages. His face is pale as he looks over at me in the hospital bed. I can see the fear in his eyes. I haven't phoned him with an update since Spencer was born. There was too much going on and I'm only starting to feel normal again now, as the effects of the drugs wear off.

"He's fine!" I say quickly, to relieve the tension.

"Where is he, can I see him?" Brendan replies. "He's in NICU. If you help me, I'll take you there."

"Should you be walking so soon?" Brendan replies, concerned.

"I'm fine, I must see him again. I'm going crazy being confined to this bed."

Five days pass before I can hold Spencer in my arms for the first time. It's emotionally overwhelming. I cry as I look down at the tiny and fragile little body. He is not much bigger now than he was at birth and his tiny body closely resembles an uncooked chicken. His chest and rib bones are prominent and there is hardly any fat on his body. *I'm terrified that I may break something if I hold him too tight.*

Spencer spent a total of 11 days in the Neonatal Intensive Care Unit. On the last day, I marched into the paediatrician's office and demanded that Spencer be released from hospital. He was no longer attached to any of the machines and I couldn't bear another day in hospital dealing with nurses that undermined and treated me like an ignorant child. I was battling to produce breast milk under those conditions. I spent every day at the hospital, from 6am each morning. Brendan usually took me home to have a shower at around 7pm, after which we both returned until one of the nurses would insist that we go home. For days I sat next to his little bed, watching over him. I insisted that they use my breast milk for the feedings, so I would use this time to pump. There was nothing that the hospital could offer Spencer that I couldn't do at home. "I'm taking my baby home today, Doctor, with or without your consent!"

CHAPTER 11

Spencer developed normally and grew into a healthy, strong and intelligent little boy. We moved to a private game reserve in the Rhenosterspruit Nature Conservancy area, a few kilometres passed Lanseria Airport. We rented a beautiful double-story thatch-house, built mainly out of stone. The house had everything one could ask for in a family home. It had a large master bedroom, with a cosy fireplace and doors that opened onto a balcony that overlooked the grass plains. The house was built on a hill and had a view over the whole area. Urbanised living was nowhere in sight. We were surrounded by nature. Game roamed freely on our front porch. My favourite was the occasional visits from a giraffe named Gigi. This was probably the happiest time of my life. I had everything I could ask for. As a little girl, I'd hoped to one day live in a game reserve. I have always been in love with the bush.

Over the months, we saved up and bought furniture to fill up our home. We invested in a flat-screen TV and a surround sound music system for the lounge. We were proud of the home environment that we had created. For the patio, we bought a table that could seat 6 people. This is where we spent most of our time, having dinner under the African sky. The stars are much brighter when they are not competing with city lights. Skye visited often and spent most weekends and holidays with us. We created many special memories together.

I worked in Bryanston as a student advisor and mentor, at a British secondary-education school that offered a distance education course to students who preferred not to attend the conventional schooling system. It took me approximately 35 minutes to get to the office. Once or twice, I arrived late for work when the herd of Wildebeest blocked the narrow sandbridge over the Crocodile River. I enjoyed working with the students and was happy with the direction my career was taking, but I couldn't wait to return home each day. If I had the choice, I would give up any job to be a stay-at-home mom, instead. I felt guilty about spending so much time away from Spencer and missing out on so much of his early-life. I earned a conservative salary, but it was enough to fulfil our needs and contribute to the payment of our expenses.

In December of 2009, we planned a holiday to the coast. We stayed over in a mountain lodge in Lesotho, an independent country in the middle of South Africa, on our way to my parents' holiday home in Umhlanga in KwaZulu-Natal. Brendan and I both thoroughly enjoy travelling and usually make a stopover in eight or nine towns on our way to any destination. Every trip is an adventure together, to explore the natural beauty of our country.

We arrive back home a few days past New Year. As we open the garage to park the car, Brendan immediately realises that something is wrong and tells me to wait in the car while he investigates.

"We've been robbed," Brendan exclaims. "Everything is gone!"

I reluctantly get out of the car to have a look at our loss. Spencer is asleep in the back of the car. I am uncomfortable even to be here. The house is a mess. Everything has been tossed out onto the floor. Every drawer and cupboard has been emptied out onto the ground. The robbers made sure not to miss anything of value. The smell of sweat lingers in each room. The smell reminds me of chopped onion. They took everything for which we had saved up and collected over time. Even the beds are stripped of all bedding and only the bare mattresses have been left. The kitchen cupboards are open and the pots, pans and cutlery are missing. I run upstairs to check the bedroom. This is where I had hidden the cameo pendant I'd inherited from my grandmother - in the back of my clothing cupboard, in a velvet jewellery bag. I cherished the pendant in memory of my gran. It's gone; they'd found it, too. They have taken most of our clothes with them and the few items that have been left behind are strewn on the floor. They'd spent time sorting through everything and selected items as one would do while shopping. I sit down in the pile of clothing for a moment to compose myself, before continuing to check the house. All the jewellery I manufactured during my studies to be a goldsmith at the Technicon of Pretoria, also has been taken, except for one small box at the bottom of the wooden Kist that managed to go unnoticed. The box has a few sterling-silver rings, a pair of earrings, a bangle and solid cross that I filed from a casted piece of silver inside it.

When it had been time to apply to universities, I told my dad that I wanted to be an artist. "I'm not going to pay for you to study, so you can end up being poor for the rest of your life!" was his response.

My dad didn't think very highly of a profession in art. I compromised by enrolling for a qualification in jewellery design and manufacturing. I reckoned that I could still express my artistic and creative flair, while satisfying my dad's business expectations by proposing to open up my own jewellery shop after I'd completed my studies. Towards the end of my second year, however, I was involved in a serious car accident in which I sustained a spinal injury. It became too difficult to manufacture, with the added strain that it put on my neck and back. After some careful consideration, I gave it up. I hated quitting. I don't give up easily.

However, if I must be honest with myself, I was never any good at manufacturing anyway. Once I almost burnt down the workshop when I used methylated spirits to quench a ring I had soldered. The flux and borax mixture was still burning when I was done. The methylated spirits caught alight and melted the plastic container in which I kept it. It ran out over the whole workbench and burnt in a bright orange flame. Everyone immediately focused their attention directly on me. It was something they had expected of me. I am a daydreamer and get lost in my thoughts; I often lose touch with my surroundings and what I'm busy with. I would never have reached much success in a manufacturing profession. I'll always look back at that time with fond memories, though. I met some of the best people I know during my student years in Pretoria.

"I don't want to be here. Let's go somewhere else!" I plead with Brendan, while softly gripping onto his arm. The house I once loved so much, that has always felt like a place I needed as a refuge, now feels breached and unsafe. "I think I'm going to be sick" and, with that, I have to leave the room. Brendan follows to talk to me.

"It won't help to run away. We were naive to think that we could leave on holiday, leave the house all by itself and not get robbed. We must be more careful from now on."

"I don't have the strength to start again from scratch. We worked so hard to get what we had.
It's so not fair!" I cry.

"Life's not fair. The sooner you make peace with that, the happier you will be." Brendan is upset too, but he hides it for my sake.

After that, it was like another spell of bad luck had come over us. The economy was not looking up and the unstable markets forced Brendan's business ventures to a grinding halt. It became increasingly difficult for him to compete with larger and stronger competitors. He took more and more financial risks out of pure desperation. He wanted to give me more; he wanted more for his children. Our financial troubles forced us to our knees.

I fell into a low state of depression. It felt like we were moving backwards in life. Everything we'd built, the life we'd created was slipping away. Every time we went out, leaving the house for even an hour, we would get robbed. After a while, we couldn't leave so much as a tin can in the kitchen cupboard without it getting stolen. We lived without a TV, without a radio, without pretty much any item of comfort, for months. After a while, the house had only our beds and sofa-set left in it. There was no point in replacing anything; it would just get taken.

The stress of the events manifested in strange physical symptoms in and on my body. Swollen, red protuberances covered each of my elbows and the inside of my mouth was speckled with white sores. Lisa, a good friend of mine, finally convinced me to go and see a doctor during my lunch hour, when I was too lethargic to focus at work one day. Lisa was also a Student Advisor. She had completed her Psychology Degree at the University of Johannesburg and was busy with her post-graduate degree studies in Special Needs Education.

"It could be lupus," Lisa says concerned. "I know someone who has it. It is when your own immune system acts up against itself. An auto-immune disorder," she explained.

I phone and get an appointment with a doctor down the road from the school. The doctor is an eccentric yet attractive woman in her mid-forties. She has long, dark, wavy hair and glowing, olivecoloured skin. She introduces herself as Dr. Macintosh.

"Have a seat, let's talk for a bit," she says and shows me to a comforter chair opposite a large desk.

Dr. Macintosh is a qualified medical practitioner but is far more interested in alternative medicine and has adopted an interesting philosophy on health.

"The mind and body are interconnected," she explains. "If your mind is right, your body will heal itself."

Dr. Macintosh asks about details of my life. "What is your relationship with your mother like?" she wants to know.

This is not at all what I expected when I agreed to seeing a doctor. It is usually a quick session of explaining your symptoms and writing a script. *I'm not sure that I'm comfortable with this session. I didn't sign up for any psych-evaluation.* It makes me very uncomfortable to speak about my family dynamics. *The matter is not about my mother. I've worked through those issues a long time ago. I'm not willing to go down that road again.*

"You have such angelic features," Dr. Macintosh says, complimenting me. "What has you this troubled? You should have the world at your feet?"

I suppose this is an attempt to make me feel more comfortable to open up towards her. It is the oldest trick in the book. Pay someone a compliment and you will have them exactly where you want them.

"I went through some things, that's all. What can I take for the inflammation on my elbows? It's quite painful and uncomfortable." I answer, to steer the conversation elsewhere.

"It is all psychosomatic. You need to get to the root of the problem." Dr. Macintosh replies.

"I guess I never took the time to deal with what happened. Everything happened so fast. I survived one crisis after the other. It's nothing serious; it will pass. Like everything else, it will pass," I explain.

Dr. Macintosh insists that I talk about it. She spends the hour listening to the abduction story and to Spencer's premature birth, then the breakins. I tell her as much as I am comfortable to discuss. She recommends me to a friend of hers, who practices traditional Chinese medicine. She explains that we need harmony in our life and mental wellness.

"Disharmony is what causes illness and disease."

Why would someone study medicine all those years, but place no trust in it? I know that I'll never actually visit her Chinese healer friend but agree to it to satisfy her. I quite like her. I find her strange, but nicer than most doctors. She is without airs or graces. I leave with a long list of prescription medications, ranging from asthma medication, antidepressants and tranquilizer tablets. Apparently, my occasional asthma attacks are also caused by stress.

Eventually we gave up the fight and moved into the cottage on my parents' property. We stayed in the cottage that they'd originally built for the staff. It took a huge financial burden off our shoulders and gave us time to reassess our lives. I had to learn how to separate myself from earthly belongings. I am sentimental and attach great value to certain possessions. Each item carried a memory and had a personal meaning to me, even if that meaning was just one of achievement. I had to teach myself to be satisfied, content and happy without these things. Attaching value to things only resulted in disappointment.

"What do we work for, then?" I ask Brendan, in a hopeless attempt to find answers. "If it can all be taken away from us, what is the point?"

"If your job makes you this unhappy, then resign, walk away," Brendan answers. "After tax and fuel, you barely make anything anyway."

It's not that I dislike my job, but I'm not sure if it's worth the sacrifice of missing out on so much of Spencer's life. I leave early each morning and get back just in time to put him to sleep.

"I've been thinking about working with birds on a full-time basis. Owls specifically. I want to open up a rehabilitation centre for them," Brendan confides. We both had realised that there is no point in doing something if it does not make you happy. When Brendan and I first decided that we would dedicate ourselves and our lives to owls, we had no idea what that would mean.

Brendan once rescued a Spotted Eagle Owl when we were staying in the Oori Game Reserve. It had a wing injury. Brendan took it to the vet, who suggested that the owl be euthanized. Brendan refused to accept that the injury wouldn't heal and convinced the doctor to give him the benefit of the doubt. Brendan's gut feeling, combined with some knowledge and experience based on his past dealings with birds of prey, was right. The owl spent 6 months with us. We named him Ozzy. Each night, we cleared the coffee table and transformed the lounge into a clinic. Changing his bandages was a challenge, dodging claws built for death. I would hold Ozzy securely in place, while Brendan would wrap up his wing in figure 8 motions.

Over time, he became comfortable with us, enough to tolerate us when we shoved antibiotic tablets down his throat. He drove in the Land Rover with us, sitting between Brendan and me on the middle storage-compartment. We took him out on field trips to fly in large, open areas, where he could regain his muscle strength and fitness ... until one day when he was strong enough and ready to survive on his own in the wild once more. We both watched in amazement as he flew off. It was a bittersweet victory. We knew that we had done all that we could for him and that it was time for him to return to where he belonged.

Ozzy had crept deep into both our hearts.

"Life is too short to waste. I want to do something that has meaning," Brendan continued.

I supported him and agreed to help him set it all up. I took over all the administration and communication duties. We registered "Owl Rescue Centre" as a Non-Profit Company at the Companies and Intellectual Property Commission and I created a website for public participation. Before long, I resigned from my job as a Student Advisor and worked from home, growing the cause. Brendan and I eloped on the 6th of November 2010. Four months later, Rebecca - our second child - was born. She had been another surprise pregnancy, but a welcomed blessing.
Brendan and I could not be happier.

We took on many different conservation and research projects. I was happy that I could focus on being a mom, while building a career at the same time.

Our first project was to install Owl Houses to create a safe breeding spot for owls in urban areas. This significantly improved the wild owl population and created a big hype around the matter of owl conservation.

We went around convincing companies to stop their use of harmful chemicals that cause secondary poisoning in non-target animals, such as owls. Instead, we offered them catch-and-release rat-traps to rent from us, with the service of collecting any rodents that they caught. This not only generated income for us, but also helped us to feed all the owls that were now in our care.

The media soon became interested in our projects and we received sponsorships and grants to help us in our quest. I sent out press releases once or twice a week, to create awareness and expand our presence on social media. The response we received was inspiring.

Before long, we needed premises for Owl Rescue Centre. When we first opened our doors as a rehabilitation centre for sick, injured and orphaned owls, an easily manageable number of owl patients and rescue calls came in every month. As we became more known in the field, more experienced and more knowledgeable on the species, the calls requesting our help started flooding in. The intake of owls was getting too large for the space we had available on my parents' property. I found an advertisement of a 'farm for sale in Hills & Dales' on the Internet and phoned up the owner to negotiate. The farm was also located in the Rhenosterspruit Nature Conservancy, but was right on the border of the Jukskei River. The river surrounded about 80% of the property. The neighbours would be close enough for us not to feel as secluded as we had felt in Oori, but far away enough for their presence not to be a burden. We signed a rental agreement, although we intended to buy a piece of the land, at a later stage, to develop the Centre.

CHAPTER 12

We moved to Hills & Dales on the 5th of August 2012 - Skye's 14th birthday. She celebrated it by inviting a few friends over to come and camp by the river. Brendan was still busy moving some of the last furniture into the house when they arrived. Nicky also stayed over that night and helped me to unpack all the boxes, while Brendan and Shayne made boerewors rolls for all of us on the braai outside.

The farmhouse was old and needed some fixing up, but it was cosy and had a certain appeal and charm to it. It was a thatched-roof house, with a loft. It was modest in size, with only two bedrooms, two bathrooms, a small kitchen and a living room. I was delighted to have a place again that we could call home and didn't care much that it was old-fashioned and unimpressive.

By this time, we had appointed four more staff members for Owl Rescue Centre. Athol was a 68year-old man, who could not survive on the pension he was earning. Zigs and Peterson were both Zimbabwean men seeking refugee status in South Africa. Brendan's son, Shayne, was the fourth person we recruited.

We erected aviaries and release enclosures all along the river, one for each species of owl. The project was growing from strength to strength. The loft area was used to raise the baby Barn Owls that came in over the winter months. In South Africa, Barn Owls typically breed from March to August of each year. It would get too cold for the small owlets outside in an aviary by the river, so the loft worked perfectly for rearing the babies. We would leave the loft windows open, so that the owls could wonder in and out as they grew and developed into fledglings. The loft served as a hack. We used a 'soft release' method to release the owls.

One Barn Owl, in particular, became very interested in our activities, paying visits to us in the bottom section of the house. We named him Barny. A wooden staircase linked the loft to our living area. He would often come and sit at the top of the stairs watching us. For hours, while we were watching TV, Barny would observe us. In time, Barny became comfortable enough to join us on the couch and became as interested as we were in the square screen, with its bright pictures and sound. Barny moved on to watch me cook in the kitchen, peeping his head into each bowl and pot. He would sit on my shoulder and watch as I worked on my laptop, turning his head in angles to study the screen. Bath time, he would land on Brendan's tummy in the bath and play in the water. He slept on the curtain-rail above my side of our bed, as if to watch over me. We never intentionally tamed Barny, or tried in any way to make him used to us. We didn't want this for the owls. We knew that he would be much better off fearing humans and staying wild. But Barny formed a special bond with our family, a relationship he favoured.

The kids developed our same passion for animals and specifically for owls that had now become our whole life. Two Spotted Eagle Owl babies were brought to us one day, barely a few days old. They had been stolen from their nest, but the people who had taken them soon realised that they had made a mistake. It is not easy to care for raptors. By this time, we could not locate the parents again and the owlets had to be raised by us, instead. People are often tempted by the idea of keeping owls as pets, but the novelty soon wears off. All that is left is hard work and a commitment often too great to handle.

Spencer was five at the time when Fluffy and Peanut came in. We name the owls only for the purpose of treatment; to keep track of who we are referring to when we discuss the owls' progress, or medical care.

Fluffy and Peanut were complete imprints. Their early interaction with humans had left an impression on them. Spencer volunteered to feed them, while Brendan and I were busy administering antibiotics, or changing bandages of other owls also in our care at the time. Rebecca would sit right next to her brother, watching in awe as the owls scoffed down the whole pieces of meat. Spencer took on this responsibility every night, until the owlets were big enough to eat on their own.

After their release, they kept returning to see the kids. We support-fed them for a period after their release, to help them to adjust in the wild. We slowly weaned them off our support and, later, watched as they hunted rats and mice for themselves. They would still come to say hello, even after a big meal and even after we had stopped feeding them. If the door was closed, we would hear a knock on the windows, a plea to get inside. Both owls would run-walk through the house and go and sit with the kids, wherever they were playing, often picking up some of their toys as if to join in.

They both eventually paired up with other owls and moved to their own territories. Their visits became less frequent. More and more owls came and went. We were rescuing between fifteen and twenty owls a month. A fellow rehabilitator from a Wildlife Rehabilitation facility we often work hand-in-hand with, once arrived at our home (which is based on the Sanctuary) with a carrier with three young Barn Owls. She looked miserable and disheartened. She had lost an owl the night before and when the second succumbed that morning, she was devastated. She got in her car and drove two hours to get to us. She was emotionally drained and needed to take a step back. I knew everything she was going through and gladly took over. A three-day-old Southern White-faced owlet, small enough to fit into a matchbox was brought to me one day. I named him Goliath. The lady who found him in her garden, where he had fallen from his nest along with his sibling, kept him longer than what she should've. She had intended to raise the owlets herself, but when Goliath's sibling died, she finally surrendered Goliath into my care. He was on the brink of death. I sat with a tiny helpless owlet, dehydrated and too weak to open its beak to allow me to feed him. I nurtured him for hours. I cried from frustration and anger towards the woman whom I believed to be accountable for his condition. I left him sleeping in a snug warm nest I had made for him. Then suddenly as if by some miracle, he reached an elevation in his progress. I could hardly believe my ears when I heard a feeding call coming from the box he was in. He was finally strong enough to eat and I knew he would be okay. There have been great triumphs in our journey; we've accomplished more than I could've imagined ever possible, we've sent thousands of owls back to the wild with a second chance at life. I have always been amazed by the determination of an owl to live and survive. Severely injured owls have survived under our care, against all possible odds, but even with the best of intentions we sometimes fail. Something that I never considered before we undertook this task, was the tremendous heartache that sometimes goes hand in hand with working with injured or sick animals and wildlife. Humans instinctively satisfy our own selfish needs before those of animals and our environment. The saddest times in my career as a conservationist is when owls come in who have been wrongfully kept as pets and harmed by the ignorance of their keepers. Owls needs specialized care and a diet that includes a high calcium phosphorus balance, vitamin and minerals. Without the correct care and husbandry, owls and other birds of prey can develop diseases including metabolic disorders. I have seen too many cases of owls suffering from MBD (Metabolic Bone Disorder), because found as young owlets they were kept as pets. I've had to hold myself back when I am handed an innocent living soul who is completely disformed with buckled legs and askew wings, with the will to live but a body that could never fulfil its function. Tears streamed down my face as I looked into the lively eyes of a Southern White-faced Owlet, who had entered this world as a perfect being but has been doomed through the selfish act of a person who thought animals can be owned like any other possession. This kind of damage is irrevocable, and we are forced into the grudging role as angelsof-death. This case of the Southern White-faced owlet had me most angry because the person who had kept the owlet, knew about our organisation. She had attended an event at our Sanctuary only months before and knew where to come for help. Instead, she decided to keep him for her own benefit, as her future companion or just something to flaunt.

I've watched as life slowly escapes bright and lively eyes, as if drawn out by some force, when the vet administers the euthanasia. He would say: "You can't save them all you know", but it never soothes the emotional turmoil within me. At times when I am exhausted from nights without much sleep and have lost a patient, self-doubt would set in. I would wonder if I am genuinely doing the right thing, if I have made the correct choices and whether I belong in this line of work at all.

There are many reasons why owls come into our Centre. Car collisions, poison, barbwire fences, diseases and persecution (something that is very prominent in South Africa due to superstitious beliefs) to name but a few. The sad reality is the significant correlation between these components that lead to owl species high mortality rate: humans. These are all man-made reasons.

Brendan always mentions the rescue he had been called out for, when a Barn Owl presumably got himself stuck in a thorn tree. He thought, "In this rare occasion it was nature that caused the harm." Only to find that even in this instance the owl who had been rung, got a thorn stuck in the ring and got caught in the process.

Besides the poisoning and injuries sustained by vehicle collisions and getting entangled in fences, we deal with many cases caused by superstition. African cultures are filled with superstition. Some fear owls as a mysterious night bird. It is seldom observed by humans, little known and often misunderstood. Some African cultures believe that if an owl hoots on your roof, it is delivering a message of death. They also associate owls with witchery. Some use owls in 'muthi', which is traditional medicine often made from animal body parts. It is believed that the consumption of these body parts can fend off disease and illness, bring fortune, or wield influence over the ancestral spirits. I was once told by a Sotho man that if you eat the eyes of an owl, it will help you to see the future. Owls are known as 'devil birds' among the majority of African people.

One time, we received a call from a company that was sponsoring our project. As part of their social investment policy, they also supported a secondary school based in Alexandra Township. A teacher had phoned them, knowing about their partnership with Owl Rescue Centre, for assistance. The owl, a Barn Owl, had gotten into the classroom and had been attacked by the whole class of students. One of its legs had been removed with a pair of scissors. The owl had succumbed to its injuries before we could get there. The students claimed that their parents and grandparents had taught them to kill these bird, whenever they saw one. The superstitions are transferred from one generation to the next and it is difficult to change these perceptions. Persecutions are still one of our biggest concerns.

I often wonder about where this fear originated and can only try to explain it in terms of an owl's unusual appearance. They have abnormally big, gazing eyes and ear tufts that resemble horns. Owls can't move their eyes inside the sockets; they are fixed by a bony structure known as a sclerotic ring, which gives the perception of staring eyes. This is also the reason that an owl can turn its head at 270 degrees.

We often rescue captured owls, in the process of being sold to witchdoctors, or from Muthi markets. The witch doctors sometimes pay up to R500 for an owl. This is a large reward to someone battling with starvation. Often, good Samaritans will buy the owls, in an attempt to rescue them. Sadly, this only encourages the trade, but it saves the lives of the owls, which leaves one with a moral dilemma. So, Brendan and I would often use their own superstitious beliefs against these superstitious followers in our educational talks. We would tell them that if they believed that owls are the messengers of death, they should also believe that owls can influence their ancestors in the afterworld. We would tell them that it is best to leave the owls and let them be, rather than to harm them. Monitoring the illegal pet trade in owls is a very important, but demanding part of our work. In one incident, we rescued two Barn Owls that had been kept in a small parrot cage for two whole years in someone's backyard. Their 'owner' had soon grown bored of his 'unusual pets' and contacted us to remove them. They were in a terrible state of health and it took over a year to rectify the damage that had been done before they could be released. Post-release monitoring played a vital role in the success of their adaption into the wild. One night, a few months after their release, we noticed an increase in their hunting activity. On closer inspection, we noticed baby owlets in the nest (Owl House). These two Barn Owls, that were once stuck in a cage, were now living a free and natural life, raising a family of their own. Brendan often gets calls to rescue owls from cell phone signal towers. The technicians of these towers are often superstitious and scared of owls, but the company also has a good policy to halt all workings where wildlife may be affected. These towers have what looks like a crow's-nest one would typically find on a ship at the top of the 30metre construction, with a door which is usually open through which the technicians can exit the tower. Barn Owls simply love these spires and often makes it their homes. What has amazed me is the owls' ability to adapt. The female would enter the door at the top and lay her eggs on the floor bottom of the tapering tower. Once the owlets hatch, the male who is the family's provider would have to bring food to mommy and babies. What is amazing, is that he never drops the food in from the top of the tower but instead, descends as if by parachute with his wings tucked above his head. To get back out, he would fly up onto the first rung of the fixed ladder and run up each rung inside the spire leaning backwards with his back pressed against the tower wall. Sometimes there would be up to twelve babies to feed and he would have to do this trip several times per night to bring enough food for each owlet and mommy. Barn Owlets can eat as much as five smallish rodents per night.

"He must be the fittest Barn Owl in the world",
Brendan would joke.

"Catching the mommy and babies for relocation is easy, but to catch him is something else."

For eight months, we lived blissfully in the countryside and proud of what the Rescue Centre had achieved. The farm was perfect for the owls. It was large and open and lush with trees. We had several successful releases and rehabilitated hundreds of owls. The project kept us busy for at least 14 hours a day. People supported the cause and we didn't have much to complain about. Things had fallen into place for us. It was not until April of 2013 that the trouble started with crime.

Peterson woke us one morning: "The skibengas (roughly translated as chancers) came. The batteries, they are all gone."

Peterson, who had come to South Africa from Zimbabwe, spoke broken English. He and Zigs lived with their families, in a commune, on the farm. Both our rescue vehicle's batteries had been stolen the night before.

That is how it started, with small petty crime. One night, Ann and Brendan's brother, Stuart, invited us to join them for a theatre production at Monte Casino. Ann is a vibrant and dynamic woman in her mid-forties. She's a businesswoman, driven and goal-orientated. Stuart is in his late forties and is laid-back and nonchalant in comparison. He allows Ann to take the lead and make most of the decisions. They started a company 15 years ago in the information technology sector that now employs roughly fifty staff. Ann drives the sales team and Stuart is the FD. The two of them have been together for just short of two decades. They have hinted along the lines of getting married, but business takes priority. The evening was planned to strengthen business relationships, so Ann had invited all her high-ranking clients. I looked forward to the event. It was the first time since we'd moved into the house at Hills & Dales that we'd had the opportunity to go out for a night on the town.

When we returned home, just shy of midnight, the house was empty. Every cupboard had been emptied out. There wasn't a pillow or a blanket left on the beds to sleep with that night. Marcia came over and lent us some bedding. It was a cold, miserable, winter's night.

Marcia and her husband Eddie were the farm managers. Marcia and Eddie's house was the first farmhouse one passed on the right-hand side of the road as one entered the farm gate. One day I was outside watching the kids play, when a police car pulled up to the house. They had taken the left split towards our house, instead of turning right to the bottom house by the river, where robbers had apparently broken in minutes earlier.

Marcia phoned us shortly after 18h00.

"Are you okay babe?" she asked concerned.

"Yes, why, what's up?" I responded, baffled. "The police were just here. The bottom house was broken into again. They stripped it bare. Even the plumbing is gone," Marcia explained. "Eddie and I are here now, chatting to the cops. Please go inside and lock your doors. It's not safe, babe."

"I know," I responded, while calling the kids to get inside the house.

"I'm staying on the line until you tell me that you are safe and locked inside," Marcia continued.

"You are acting a little paranoid, Marcia, more so than normal." I mocked. "Bye, we are safe, don't worry about us. Thanks for the call. We'll see you tomorrow."

As I put down the phone, Brendan came walking into the kitchen with his phone in his hand.

"Just phone Marcia there. Peterson has just phoned to say that they are breaking into madala's house." Madala means old man, which was what the farm workers called Eddie. "Peterson could see the robbers from the commune."

"No, he must have it wrong, I was just on the phone with Marcia. They were busy talking to the cops just outside their house when I spoke to her. The bottom house was broken into." I replied, confused.

"Let's go see what is going on. They may need help," Brendan answered.

We told the kids to get into the car, quickly. On our way over, three gun shots went off. Eddie screamed so loud that it echoed through the farmland: "You bloody bastards! I'll kill you! You bloody bastards!"

Two assailants had broken into Marcia and Eddie's place, with the police parked only metres away. They had jumped through the window, stolen the TV and laptop and had run off.

Marcia and Eddie packed up and moved out over the next few days. They were disgruntled over their loss. They had paid installments for their TV over many months of labour. They were both qualified electricians, or 'sparkies', as we refer to them in jargon, and had worked a hard, honest day to make ends meet.

A week after Marcia and Eddie moved out, on the Thursday night, we hear a shotgun go off and, moments later, Peterson and his wife Di are at our door.

"They have big guns!" Peterson shouts. He is trembling with fear. Di is in shock. She is unable to speak. Brendan unlocks the security-gate to let them in. Peterson continues to explain how the attackers had shot through their door. The bullet had come in through the door and penetrated through the back wall. Peterson and his wife had escaped through the back window and ran straight to our house for protection and shelter.

Di and I hide upstairs in the loft with the kids, while the men are downstairs keeping watch for any further activity.

"How many are there Di?" I want to know. "Eish, I don't know, six or seven or eight maybe."

I go cold. *How do we defend ourselves and our kids against possibly eight armed men?*

I phone Marcia, who I know is someone I can count on for help, even though they had moved off the farm and are no longer the caretakers. Marcia and Eddie are both kind and selfless friends. My hands are shaking so much that I can hardly keep the phone to my ear. I whisper to her over the phone, petrified to be discovered by the armed thugs. Marcia has a contact at Erasmia Police Station. She phones the Superintendent on his cellphone.

I was about 20 years of age when I lost my faith in the police force. I was renting a one-bedroom cottage on a small farm in Muldersdrift, not far from my old primary school, at the time. One night, around 9pm, screeching tyres broke the silence of the quiet, country night. The sound was followed up shortly by the terrified scream of a woman. An accident, I thought. Minutes later, three gun shots went off. I immediately ran to grab my cell phone and dialled 10111 to call the police. On the other side of the phone call sat an uninterested woman.

"What crime has been committed, ma'am?" she'd asked indifferently.

I explained the scream and gunshots. At very least, a vehicle collision. Someone was in trouble; of that I was sure.

"I'll see if I can find a vehicle to send, ma'am."

At that point I was pleading with the lackadaisical woman, who was clearly only interested in her monthly pay cheque. As the call continued, the screams of the woman were becoming louder and more compelling. I could hear her pain. It was unlike anything I had ever heard before. A horrendous, chilling noise. I continued pleading and started explaining the exact location and direction from which the commotion was coming. Fifteen minutes passed before I phoned again. Another incompetent individual was on the line. Fifteen minutes after that and there was still no siren. Nothing, but dead quiet. Well after midnight, I was woken by a phone call - three hours after my last contact with the police. It was a cop on the line, wanting to get a statement from me.

"I cannot open for you at this time of the morning. I don't know anything more than the information I gave you over the phone. If you want me to give you a formal statement about what I heard, you should return at a decent hour,"

I responded to the phone call, annoyed. "Can you tell me what it is that you need from me?" I asked before ending the conversation.

"There has been a homicide, ma'am," the officer replied.

Shocked, I put down the phone. I could not sleep for the rest of the night. A friend later told me that a newspaper article had reported on the incident. A young couple had tried to avoid a stack of rocks in the middle of the road, which had caused an accident. The killers, who had planted the rocks, had sat waiting for their unsuspecting victims. The husband had been shot and killed and his wife had been raped and had then suffered a less merciful death. She had been beaten to death with a steel pipe. The reason for this cruel death remains unknown.

I had heard every distressing scream. The thought of it had haunted me for weeks on end. For nights, I'd lain awake, thinking about her and her suffering... and had cried myself to sleep. I was
so disgusted by this representation of the human race.

"You will just have to wait it out. Help is on its way," Marcia says, trying to console me.

As promised, a police van arrives minutes later. We all get into the car to go and meet them.

"Are they the police, Mommy?" Spencer wants to know.

"Yes, my boy. They are here to help."

"Will they take the baddies away, Mommy?" he continues curiously.

"I hope so sweetie, I really hope so."

A few weeks later I was crossing the river, on my way back from fetching Spencer from school. I always took the short road to the farm, across a shallow bridge over the river, passed Jan's place. I could only take this road when it hadn't been raining and the river was low. To the left, the river curved and bent around, to run parallel to the road.
At the river-bend, many crossed through from Malatjies to Diepsloot. This was also where the troublemakers crossed over to gain access to the farms. The farm workers also used this crossing. On that day, four men were fishing there. They had cast a net into the river, with two men on either side to hold it in place.

When I drove past, there were police vehicles parked all along the riverbed. Police divers were in the river, searching for something.

The next morning, Lydia, a Zimbabwean lady who helped me around the house, told me that a giant snake had come from the water and grabbed the fishermen.

"They are the ones who have been robbing in the area," she said. "The other people saw them disappearing into the river."

Peterson spoke of a mermaid, instead - a sorceress, who was half-human and half-fish. She took victims who made her angry.

The police retrieved two bodies from the river. One of the men's fingerprints matched those taken from crime scenes in the area. In one of the robberies, a farmer had been brutally murdered and his wife had been tied up and tortured. The robbers had forced the farmer's wife to open the safe and had left with firearms and ammunition. On that night, their Jack Russel had been barking and sniffing at the front door. After a while, the farmer had gotten up from in front of the TV to let the dog out. As he'd opened the door, he'd been gunned down in cold blood.

For weeks after the double drownings, there was no more crime in the area. Those who believed the story, stayed completely clear of the river. They took the long way home. Lydia was one. She was terrified of the creature. Its legend was a big part of conversation in the settlement. All the workers on the farm were cautious of the water.

The belief spread wide and far. Everyone told the story of a mystical river creature, only with a few variations.

The truth about what had happened there that day still remains unknown.

CHAPTER 13

We fed the owls the same time every night, blowing on a whistle, as the food was placed on the feeding platforms - a classical conditioning method we adopted in our tried-and-tested release technique. The owls become conditioned to associate the sound of the whistle with the prey with which they were provided. Long after the release, Brendan would whistle and the owls would return during feeding sessions. Those who struggled to hunt at first, were support-fed, whilst they slowly adapted back to their normal and natural existence. This is how we monitored the success of each release.

Some nights, a parliament of owls gathered in the trees surrounding the house, all coming for easy prey. It was quite a sight to see as they gathered one by one, as if to prepare for a presiding of sorts. They sat gazing with content confidence and perfect poise, as they patiently waited for the prey. If you have ever found yourself lucky enough to stare into the eyes of an owl, you will understand why some people feel intimidated in the presence of this unique and majestic bird. To be surrounded by so many of them is an exhilarating feeling of being; it's as if they can gaze straight into your soul, to where even your deepest of secrets are exposed and laid bare.

Once we were sure that the owls were hunting enough to sustain themselves, we weaned them off our support. Watching them return to the wild has always been the best part of the job.

The 17th of July 2013 was a quiet Thursday evening. The wind that could usually be heard howling through the old farmhouse was silent and calm on this night. This hauntingly eerie sound, to which we fell asleep most evenings, was completely absent from the dark atmosphere.
Even the owls were quiet, not a hoot or a screech. Most had moved on to find their own territories. Their visits had become infrequent.

Brendan was cutting up day-old chickens for the young juvenile Spotted Eagle Owls and the Pearl Spotted Owl we had in the aviaries. He had unlocked the security-gate and placed food on the platform, should some of the released owls decide to come. Only the owls in the aviaries still needed feeding.

Rebecca had fallen asleep on our bed shortly after dinner. I helped Spencer get ready for bed. I ran the bath in the ensuite bathroom of our bedroom, while keeping a watchful eye on Rebecca. She was developing a slight cold and I was worried that it would turn serious. Her temperature frequently shot up while she was asleep.

We had strict rules about bedtime, especially on school nights. It was a little later than Spencer's regular bath time, but he had helped to feed the dogs first. Spencer was five years old, but years ahead for his biological age, and was therefore given responsibilities that were not typical for a boy of his age. He was busy getting undressed when Brendan came in to wash his hands and to rinse his knife in the basin, whilst making small talk about the serrating on the blade.

Brendan turned around to leave the bathroom to continue with the feeding but, as he took a few steps from the bathroom towards the exit of the bedroom, before he could reach the bedroom door, he bellowed out in an unnerved, shuddering tone. I knew straight away, from the sound of his voice, that something was terribly wrong. I heard his immediate plea: "PLEASE, NO!" he implored. Somehow I knew exactly what to expect next.

It wasn't the same panic-stricken cry one would expect if he was being confronted by a 6' foot Snouted Cobra, hissing with a warning hood. We were confronted by those often. Nor was it the sound that would come from a man who didn't think that his life and that of his family was in severe danger. This was the desperate sound of a man, who believed that his life was about to end. A despairing cry. But Brendan didn't scream for himself, he screamed for his children … for his tiny little girl who was lying sound asleep on the bed less than a metre away; for his young and innocent boy; and for me, his wife whom he loved and had vowed to protect.

Brendan is now pushed back into the bathroom, with the muzzle of a large shotgun pressed tightly against him, securely resting in his ribs. A tall, robust, dark man is holding onto the stock at the other end of the gun, his finger in place, softly gripping the trigger.

I only glance at him for a second and then turn to Spencer to help him put his clothes back on. My hands are moving fast, but clumsily. Spencer is confused. He's tired and doesn't understand what is happening, so he resists and wants to get into the bath.

"Just put your clothes on for now. Please do as Mommy says."

"On the floor!" the man's command issues forth in a harsh tone, "Look down. If you look up, I'll shoot!"

I can hear by his voice that he's nervous. Nervous people usually makes stupid mistakes. One's cognitive ability is impaired when one is uneasy in a situation. This scares me. *Coward! He comes and picks on a family with small, innocent children. Weak excuse of a human being.* I'm trembling.

A million thoughts have entered my mind at the same time.

"Screw you! Screw you!" I shout inside my head, while my outer appearance remains completely unchanged and still. *"Screw you for coming into my home and callously taking what I earned through hard work. Screw you for poisoning my thoughts and my life, while you continue to exist like pollution."*

The three of us are sitting in a row against the side of the bath. The bath was raised one level higher than the bathroom floor, with a step to get in. We are sitting shoulder to shoulder, legs crossed and our heads tilted down into our laps. I'm in the middle. With my body, I try to shelter Spencer by pushing a little in front of him, tilting slightly sideways. The robber has the gun pointed down at us.

Will my body stop the bullet?

Brendan had dropped his knife on the floor as he had sat down. I now picked it up and, with a slow, sliding movement, place it behind my back. I grip onto it, squeezing my fingers over the handle until my knuckles turn white. And then release it again, toying with the idea of using it when the time comes.

If I pass it to Brendan, will he be able to overpower the thug? How do we get out of this situation? What is the robber's plan with us? Is he alone?

"Come in, my friends!" the robber shouts towards the bedroom door. My heart drops for a second time.

How many are there?

"Where are the laptops? Where are you hiding your cell phones?" the assailant impatiently wants to know.

Nobody else has entered.

Was he just bluffing? He has a South African accent. He's definitely a local.

There had been (and still continues to be) some trouble with foreigners crossing our borders from other African countries, coming here for better prospects, but if they aren't able to find any, they turn to a life of crime and steal instead. The situation with illegal immigrants has become completely out of hand. In the past, some communities have become so upset with the foreigners that they have resorted to violence. The illegal refugees who flood the country daily, climbing fences and crossing rivers, either threaten the job security of the legal citizens, or contribute to the already perturbing epidemic of crime in the country. Xenophobic attacks are what the media calls them. If the citizens catch a foreigner, during this phase of attacks, they simply tie him up, place a tyre around his neck and set it alight. Burning people alive. No questions asked. No proof of any crime required. This is a common practice in informal settlements, known as necklacing. People are necklaced for many different reasons. This is how the community of these informal settlements deals with people who they believe have wronged them in some way. A mob of people all join in to serve 'justice'. Mob justice. It is lawless, but I can reluctantly understand their motives.

But this is a Xhosa man.

He calls for his friends to join him once more. Nobody comes. They are probably nervous about the owls. *I wish Barny would fly in for a visit.*
Barny used to fly up high and come down, using all his body weight to pounce on the head of any person who wasn't part of the family. He did this to Jan once, when he came over for coffee. *That would get rid of him.*

There is also no sign of Cleo, our Chow, who is usually the best guard dog. People are afraid of her. She is a loyal and faithful dog. *I hope they didn't harm her.*

Rubi, a little cross-breed puppy we rescued, is barking her biggest and bravest bark at the intruder. He pays no attention to her.

"Sweetie, tell him where the laptop is," Brendan says anxiously, hoping that this is all he has come for. I start explaining that he should leave the bedroom and look behind the counter that is around the corner. This is where I sit and work, answering emails from people looking for advice and help with owls. People from all over the world contact us for assistance with injured birds. I pack away the laptop in its bag every night, once I've finished doing what I've had to do for the day. There are no curtains covering the small window in the door that leads into that area of the house from the outside and I don't want anyone to be able to look through the window and spot the laptop, so I always pack it away and place it out of sight underneath the counter. The paintball handgun that Brendan had bought me, should the time ever come when I'd need to defend myself, is also in the laptop bag. I keep it loaded with pepper-gas bullets.

The robber becomes impatient. He does not understand my instructions. His voice turns harsh and violent. I try to explain again, but I can tell that he is not paying any attention. He is probably too nervous to process the information. I become uneasy with his splenetic manner and insist that he will find it where I have explained it is.

At times, he is almost pleasant. Using words like

'please' to ask for things and addressing me as Ma'am. He assures me that he is not there to hurt us … if we give him what he wants. I can tell that he is uncomfortable and wants to get out of there fast. Something has him very unsettled. This makes him lose his cool.

"The boy must fetch it!" he shouts, referring to Spencer.

"No, I'll go. Let me do it." I beg and plead, while staring up at him, looking straight into his eyes. "Don't look at me!" the command comes fast, as he aims the muzzle at my face.

I quickly back down and gaze at the ground, while still pleading with him not to involve our children. I have looked at him long enough to recognise his face, though. I have seen him before, but I cannot place him. I scramble my brain to try and work it out.

He is a large man. He wears a big, black jacket, with an orange-tiger logo sewn onto the left breast area, and a black beanie is pulled over his head, down to his eyebrows. He has a broad face and neck and a very dark complexion. His eyes are small and his nose is flat and wide. His ears are positioned high up on his head and only the tip of his earlobes are visible under the beanie. He has long facial hair, thinly spread over his beard area. Long, curly hairs protrude from his chin. I am good at remembering faces. I am an artist and enjoy drawing portraits. When I look at someone, I notice facial proportions, bone structure and precise detail. A photographic image configures in my memory.

When I meet someone, I always associate him or her with an animal. The symbol helps me to group people into certain categories of character and traits, from where I can decipher their inner-being to gain a certain understanding of who they may be. Like the fisherman Brendan and I met fishing, out on the walkway along the river one day. He immediately struck me as a snake. He was friendly, intelligent and seemingly kind, but he had a shifty undertone to his character. It was just a hunch and I couldn't explain the association I had drawn between him and this specific creature. Months later, Brendan involved him in one of our projects and, sure enough, over time, he showed this side of his personality, which explained why I'd initially imaged him as a snake. He was deceitful and dangerously manipulative.

My kids are little monkeys, inquisitive, playful and somewhat mischievous. This man, with shotgun in hand, is seen by me as a gorilla. He is large, strong, broad-shouldered and very dark in appearance, towering over us like a giant rather than a man. He has raging outbursts of temper, and I can almost imagine him pounding on his chest to enforce his dominance. Then, there are quiet moments, when I picture him as sympathetic and a bit more docile. *He is nervous about me looking at him. Is he someone familiar? Someone I have encountered before?*

"The boy must get it. Do as I say, if you want to keep your family alive!" he commands, still unnerved.

I turn to Spencer and gently place my hands on either side of his slim upper arms.

"It will be okay. You know where Mommy keeps her laptop. Go with the man and show him where it is. Then come straight back to Mommy."

My heart wants to leap from my chest. I start counting the seconds. I'll only give him a few seconds to return. Then I'll go after them.

1, 2, 3, 4, 5, 6, 7, 8.... 15.

Spencer returns. I look up for another brief second. The robber has my laptop-bag draped over his shoulder. His body posture is arrogantly slouched. Spencer sits back down next to me. I take his tiny little hand and hold it in mine, slightly squeezing.

You are only five. My brave, courageous little boy.
The world sure is a cruel place.

"Now, tell me where your cellphones are." Brendan starts explaining, willing him to leave us in peace and not to make any further demands.

"It's on the counter in the TV room."

"They are both there," I add, "but mine is probably on the couch."

He threatens that he will harm us if he finds that we are not being truthful.

A sound can be heard coming from the loft.

"Are you alone here?" the assailant utters.

No, no we are not alone.

Since the incident at the staff compound, when Peterson and his wife Di came to us for help, they have all moved into our house and have been living upstairs in our loft. They were too afraid to return to their rooms, where they felt vulnerable to another attack. The area was cleaned out and Peterson, Di, Pieter, Brigadier and Brigadier's wife brought their beds and all their personal belongings to the top area of our home.

"No," I stress to the armed man, "there are a few guys living in the upstairs section of the house." Until this moment, I'd forgotten that they were there. I feel slight relief; less isolated.

Within a few minutes, he is gone. Brendan follows right behind him and shuts the bedroom door. He grasps Rebecca from our bed, takes her in his arms and runs back to the bathroom. He swiftly locks the bathroom door and hands Rebecca to me.

"Get into the bath, stay clear of the door. He may shoot through it. You will be safest in the bath behind the wall, which will provide cover from a bullet." "What do we do now?" I ask in dismay.

I know Brendan has a plan. He always does. If someone can get us out of this situation, it will be him. "Put on your shoes and get ready to run. I'll take Spencer. Will you be okay with Rebecca?"

"Yes," I nod. I mentally prepare myself, as we are about to run for our lives.
Brendan picks up the heavy porcelain toilet-tank cover and smashes it through the narrow, vertical bathroom window that is next to the bath. Rebecca lets out a hysterical scream, gasps for air and then starts crying. Within a flash, without giving it a second thought, we both dive through the broken glass shards in the window-pane. I keep Rebecca's head tightly tucked into my chest, as I bound through the sharp glass pieces left

behind in the frame. She cries as we run. We head straight towards the river to find shelter.

Blood is streaming down my face. I wipe it away while I run, to keep it from blocking my sight. I retch as the blood that gushes from the wound enters my mouth. Rebecca cries out to Brendan.
He stops to take her from me. "Dadda, Dadda, Mommy eina."

He now has a child clutching onto each of his arms. Spencer won't run by himself. He is scared and confused.

"Keep going!" I urge Brendan on.

"You are bleeding. Are you okay to run?"

"Get the kids to a safe spot, I'm right behind you," I respond, without hesitation. When it comes to protecting my children, I would run even if one of my legs had been cut off.

The riverbank is brightly lit under the moon. We are vulnerable and exposed.

"There, the washed-up log, we can fit the kids underneath it," I whisper to Brendan, anxious to remain unnoticed. We make our way to the huge, heavy tree trunk that was brought in by a flood a few weeks before. It is securely anchored on the sandbank, with a hollow big enough to squeeze into.

"Stay here with the kids, I'll be back shortly," Brendan instructs.

"No, don't leave us, please just stay," I plead.

"I'm bringing the car to fetch you. We need to get out of here. You probably need stitches for that wound."

"That means fetching the keys from the house?!" I respond in a panic.

"I can get in and out undetected. Trust me, it will be okay. Besides, if I'm by myself, I only have to worry about myself, instead of trying to protect everyone. He has a shotgun. Reloading takes a lot of time. He only has one shot and chances are that he won't be very accurate. I'll be back before you know it. Stay strong and look after Spencer and Rebecca. Run if you must. Keep your eyes peeled."

Spencer has a lot of questions. He is puzzled by our behaviour. "Why are we waiting here? Where is Daddy going? I want to go sleep."

"Shhhh, we have to be quiet." My voice trembles as I try to calm him.

"Is that the police mommy? What did he want your laptop for?"

"No sweetie, that is a very bad man. He stole it from us. We can't let him find us. Do you understand?"

"But Mommy, he wears the same clothes as the police do. I thought he came to help us." "Shhhhhh, Mommy will talk to you just now. For now, we have to be very quiet. Like when we play hide and seek. Understand?"

Please let Brendan be okay. Please let us get out of here.

A bright light shines up on the horizon. That must be Brendan. A craggy pathway leads almost right up to where we've taken cover.

If we time it correctly, we will be out of here within minutes. The grant purple SsangYong Musso we picked up for a bargain when we desperately needed a 4 x 4 vehicle for one of our projects, pulls up with a missing left headlight.

"Sorry, sweetie, I bumped the car. I tried to get it out of there fast and missed a tree."

"You mean you *didn't* miss the tree," I respond, with a slight grin. I'm relieved to be out of that assailable position and couldn't care less about the condition of the car.

"Well, let's just say I didn't see the tree."

"Where do we go now? It's late at night. I don't want to trouble anyone at this time."

"I thought about dropping the kids at my mom, but she may go into a panic over the whole thing. The last thing I want to do is wake her like this."

"I agree."

"We'll have to go to my brother's house. It will be safe there and it's close to a hospital. Dial his number for me."

"You got your phone...?"

"Yes, I grabbed it off the counter when I fetched the keys. Have you lost a lot of blood?" Brendan asks, concerned.

"No, it looks worse than it is. A head injury tends to bleed a lot, but the cut isn't serious."

The kids fall asleep in the back of the car as we drive. It is a 40-minute trip to the opulent golf security-estate in Johannesburg, where Stuart and Ann reside. A security code is required to enter the estate and a whole process of proper identification is involved, before they will let us enter. I use my sweatshirt to clean up my face, trying to appear normal as we queue under an intense spotlight to enter the estate. Dolled-up, wealthy women flash their residency cards in the right lane to enter without delay, glaring over to our side. They live behind high walls, electric fences and security-gates.

They know nothing about my world. Wealthy people have the benefit of removing themselves from certain circumstances, conditions and surroundings. To some extent, freedom is for sale.

I slide down in the seat, somewhat embarrassed by my appearance. Ashamed for being a victim of the lifestyle I have chosen.

Stuart is at the door within seconds to receive us. "Sjoe, Pop, are you okay?" he asks, disturbed.

"I am now. Thank you." My words are few. I am very emotional. "Can you help Brendan to take the kids upstairs?" Ann takes me to their room to clean the wound and takes out a pair of her pyjamas for me to put on. "Are you sure you don't want it checked out by a doctor? Maybe have it stitched?"

"No, it will be fine. I don't feel like going anywhere right now."

In the background, I listen to Brendan relay the story. I can still hear the shock in his voice. Tonight, has really scared him. I take comfort in the fact that we are now miles away from danger. We have made it out. And my family lives to see the next sunrise.

CHAPTER 14

The kids and I stayed with Ann and Stuart's for just short of a month. Brendan came to visit often, but could not leave the farm for long periods. He knew that if he did, we would lose every last bit of our possessions. I could not handle that - starting all over again. The farm workers wouldn't stay there without him, either. They depended on his protection. Besides, he had the owls to take care of. He did not take this responsibility lightly.

This was one of the most trying periods of my life. Every night he slept away on the farm, a grim fear gripped my limbs and would not leave until the morning. I hated the emptiness of the bed.

On the Sunday night after the attack, the thugs returned to the farmhouse. Whether it was the same ones, or another group, Brendan couldn't say for sure. He expected that they would come. These incidents never happened singly. The word would have gotten out that we had vacated the place.

They practice tactics of alienation, chasing people from their houses. They then strip the houses clean until there is nothing left to take. When the last copper pipe and cables are stolen, the building is burnt to the ground. We have seen this happen all around us.

Cleo, our chow-chow, stayed on the farm with Brendan. She sat up all night, staring into the darkness, looking out through the glass-pane window of the kitchen door. It was like she knew that danger was lurking in the shadows of the dubious and perilous nocturnal atmosphere that took over shortly after sunset. She was as suspicious of the darkness as were we. There were very few quiet nights.

Brendan waited them out. He no longer saw them as human beings. They acted with pure cruelty. He viewed them as diabolic creatures, without cognitive ability or reason, behaving like wild animals, on instinct and drive alone. They were murdering, raping and plundering. His normal human-compassion was removed from his perception of these savage criminals. Whether these crimes were committed out of poverty, or whether as a result of years of oppression, the cruel method in which they were committed was reprehensible.

Cleo raises his suspicion. He sees her body posture change. He signals her not to bark. A gunshot is fired in the direction of the house. They are testing to see if someone is home. They wait for retaliation before they strike. Brendan waits patiently. He wants a clear shot. Three men appear from the darkness, within range of the back door light. Brendan is lying flat on his stomach, peeping through the narrow window, armed

and ready for attack. Slightly driven by vengeance, he plans his next move. They move closer. Cleo gets uncomfortable with the closing distance between the assailants and the house. She goes against Brendan's command and lets out a baleful bark.
It's enough to scare them off.

For three weeks, they kept coming back. Sometimes every second night. Sometimes as many as four silent nights would pass. But they kept coming back. Brendan waited, night after night.

Wayne, a friend of the landlord, moved into the cottage where Marcia's daughter used to live. They'd moved out shortly after the first attempted break-in that threatened their security. He was asked to assist with safeguarding the farm. The cattle, livestock and buildings all had become a concern. Wayne was ex-military, middle-aged and recently had been retrenched. He was short and stocky, with calves that could probably kick-start a Boeing. His bad eating and drinking habits revealed themselves in the added abdominal fat he carried like a pregnant woman. Wayne's motherin-law had moved into his house not long after he'd lost his job and, to escape her continuous scolding about his unemployed status, he spent 5 days a week on the farm. He told his wife that he was busy on a project. That satisfied her. She couldn't stand him being jobless, sitting around the house doing nothing. Instead, Wayne now sat for twenty hours a day, in a chair on the stoep of the small cottage overlooking the farmland, with a shotgun in one hand and a glass of Tassenberg red wine in the other. He shot at anything that moved. He had gone through harsh and specialised training in his heyday, but this situation frightened him. Brendan enjoyed his company, as he had good stories to tell. Having another person on the farm helped. Wayne was trigger-happy. This kept most intruders at bay. So, they stopped coming for a while.

When Lynn and her husband couldn't take the lifestyle anymore, Neil moved into the farmhouse on the riverbend at the bottom of the farm. His daughter and her husband moved into Marcia and Eddie's old place. A contractor was employed to fix it up after it had been ransacked. Brendan went over to introduce himself. He warned them about the security issue, something he wished someone had done for us, but they seemed uninterested. They had 12 horses and 17 dogs and were no strangers to farm living. Neil looked like an unkempt jockey, short and slender. He was cocky and used offensive language to express his opinion. A deranged gunslinger. A cowboy.

One evening, at around 6pm, Neil's daughter was left by herself in the farmhouse near the gate. Her husband had gone over to Neil's place for a drink. She was relaxing in the bath when three men entered the house. They pulled her from the bath and tied her up, naked.

In her bare and vulnerable state, they mocked and harassed her, taking pleasure in her vulnerability and humiliation. They left with the TV and a few insignificant items. She suffered an epileptic attack during the ordeal and people who knew her said that she was never the same again after this.

Neil went berserk. He professed that he would find them and make them pay for what they had done. He pledged to hunt them like animals and feed their corpses to the pigs he kept in the kraal near his house.

The circumstances had people do and say things that were frightening, unthinkable and insane.

I spent my days searching everywhere for another place we could move to. The area had a particularly grave standing and migration seemed like the only reasonable option we had left, in order to protect our family from any further anguish.

To our friends and family, it seemed simple; we could choose to live like everyone else in a security-estate, or housing complex. But to us, this wasn't duck soup.

For my ninth birthday my sister bought me a storybook about two mice, one who lived in the countryside and one who lived in the city. The country mouse received a letter from his cousin who lived in the big city, informing him of his visit. Country Mouse went straight to work, preparing for his very special guest. He caught a fish for lunch, made salad freshly picked from his garden and made apple pie with apples picked from his apple tree. City Mouse arrived in a flashy, red sports car. After lunch, he thanked Country Mouse for the very nice, but conservative meal and then invited him to experience the lavish life of the city, instead. He felt pity towards the poor country mouse and his simplistic existence. The trip to the city was stressful to Country Mouse, who was used to a tranquil and calm life. The buzzing of traffic made him anxious. They had to dodge fast cars, huge trucks and drove through puffs of smoke. When the two mice arrived in the city, there was a sumptuous meal waiting for them. A variety of meats, vegetables, roast potato... more than the two mice could dream of eating. Dinner, however, was soon interrupted by a cat. The two mice had to flee from the beastly mouser and hide in an uncomfortable small hole in the wall. When the cat was nowhere to be seen, the country mouse thanked his cousin and left to return to the countryside. "You do, indeed, live in a plentiful city, but I'm going home where I can enjoy my dinner in peace," Country Mouse told City Mouse.

I have always been that country mouse. I don't fancy the bright lights of the city. I enjoy the smell of wet soil just after a rainstorm. I enjoy the crisp taste of freshly-picked peas. I like to see nothing but darkness and bright stars when I look out at night. But this perfect picture is now spoiled by savage farm attacks.

Life turned into a quandary. We couldn't move to a townhouse in a security-complex. We would not fit in there. Brendan and I are not made to be city slickers. No one can guarantee our safety there, either. But the farm lands are targeted; we know this. We needed space for the owls, so this meant taking that risk. We had built a life around the Rescue Centre. It had become who we are. Just like a farmer's oneness and livelihood is in his produce and in his land; he cannot be expected to part from it. Finding a farm at the price that we could afford, and that offered a form of security, was almost impossible.

My life seemed to have become an inescapable world of gathering darkness. I felt overwhelmed by the fear that had me at its mercy. It made me desperate.

In one of my searches, I found an ad for a bushveld farm, with a small lodge, for sale in an area close to Hartbeespoort Dam in the North-West Province. The owner was a man named Roger. I phoned him and he seemed happy to negotiate. He'd had it on the market for some time. Very few people were buying large tracts of land under the prevailing circumstances. It was advertised as a 45ha piece of land, fully enclosed by electric fence - this meant a form of security - with a few chalets and tents. He wanted R5 500 000 for it at

the time. We went to look it at. It was a beautiful bushveld environment. It would be perfect for the owls and, with the accommodation that we could provide, it had the potential for us to be able to grow our education projects. But the buildings were rundown and needed a lot of work. Brendan proposed to Roger - with a full disclosure of our
position - that we fix it up and thereafter rent it on a month-to-month basis. Roger, uncompromising by nature, seemed offended by our offer and, in his sentiment for the property, didn't take to our proposal. Two years later, we would meet with Kobus, an estate agent in the area, who would reopen the negotiations between Roger and ourselves. But until then, we carried on living on the farm in Hills & Dales.

On the 9th of August, Ann invited me along to a Woman's Day networking lunch for driven and successful businesswomen. I had no interest in going, but it seemed important to Ann, so I faked my enthusiasm. *Who knows, I may even surprise myself and enjoy the whole affair.* I was eternally grateful to Ann and Stuart for taking us in and making us feel welcome in their home. I had come to know Ann as a caring and generous person with a strong desire to uplift those around her. So, I felt obliged to attend, although she may just have been polite when she asked me to join her. She seemed excited to introduce me to a few of her collaborators.

The luncheon was hosted at a glamorous venue in Sandton. The tables were elegantly set for three hundred attending guests. The guest speaker at the prestigious event was an inspiring, young and attractive girl with a tragic story.

I was seated with nine capitalist businesswomen, with whom I had very little in common. My recent experience had left me withdrawn and unsociable. In my bitterness towards the outside world, I had little desire to chit-chat with a table of goal-driven individuals, all trying their utmost to outshine one another. I preferred to be left alone altogether. My hopes and my dreams all seemed lost now, and I resented them for (what I perceived as) living perfect, uncomplicated lives. Instead, I sat quietly listening to the young, pretty, soft-spoken, 25year-old brunette tell her harrowing recollection of the day that she was gang-raped. She had been with her dad, walking their dogs in a park in Durban, not far from where they lived, when a group of men had approached them. She'd remembered passing them and greeting them earlier that afternoon. They'd seemed harmless, friendly even. The men had caught them offguard. Her dad had been badly beaten and had been made to watch as the gang of immoral, young men had each, in turn, raped his daughter. The hat that he had worn on his head had been shoved down his throat with a knife, to stifle his agonising pleas. The young girl told of her experience, in vivid detail, about how they had forced her to the ground, how they had pulled down her panties and had laughed as she'd cried out in pain. She had subsequently created a foundation to support rape survivors. After months of counselling, she had empowered herself through public motivational speaking. Telling her story had helped her to overcome the power it had had over her. She now wanted to give other women - other rape victims - hope to help them to carry on with their lives, after the suffering.

"This happens to a woman in South Africa every 17 seconds," she explained.

I sat there, inconsolable. What had happened to my country, a country I love so much? All I could think about was my own daughter. The thought was unbearable. And there, for the first time, I appreciated what people had meant when they'd said I was lucky. I felt ashamed that it had angered me before when they'd said it. I hadn't been myself for a very long time. The encounters had alienated me from who I am in my essence; they had threatened my inner security. I was at risk of losing my innocuousness. I couldn't see past my anger about the wrong that had been done to me, to my family. I failed to see all the hurt that was out there, all around me, experienced by people every day. I had become selfish and self-concerned. I was impatient to get back to Ann's house, where Brendan was waiting. I told him that I wanted to go home. It was time. I missed him. I missed our home.

"We won't be unprepared this time. We'll never be unsuspecting victims again."

Flight or fight, those were the options. Until we had somewhere else to go, fight was the only option. I was done with hiding away. I was done with allowing the fear to take over my life. It was time to go home.

Danelle's parents, Hendrik and Renè, two weeks after the armed robbery friends manage to persuade them to attend a braai.

From left: Skye, Danelle and Spencer in 2008.

Brendan and Danelle when they first started dating.

A curious mongoose peaks over Brendan's shoulder while he is on a phone call with a radio station.

Brendan with a Spotted Eagle Owl in Hills & Dales.

Fluffy, a Spotted Eagle Owl raised by Spencer (aged 5 here), comes to visit him.

Brendan with Rebecca, a month after the armed robbery in Hills & Dales.

Danelle with Barny the Barn Owl.

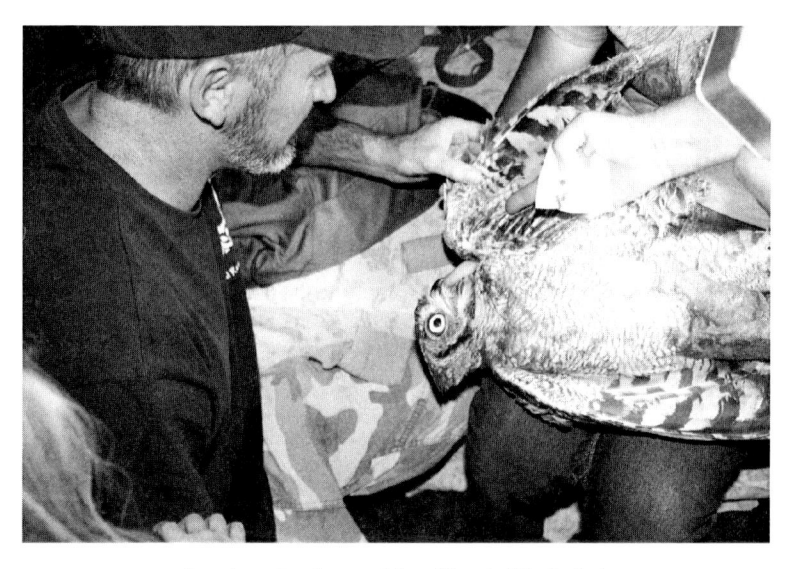

Brendan attends to an injured Spotted Eagle Owl.

Danelle with Zoey the Zebra.

Brendan rescues a Spotted Eagle Owl with an injured wing.

A drawing Danelle created from a photograph she took of a Southern White-faced Owl that was in their care at the time.

Rebecca holds a Pearl Spotted Owlet.

A photograph taken by Danelle from inside one of the enclosures at the Centre.

A released Spotted Eagle Owl returns to a feeding platform within the Owl Sanctuary at Hartbeespoort.

Brendan release a Marsh Owl, rescued from a Muthi market, into an enclosure at the Centre.

Danelle and Brendan in Wilderness, where they would undertake a yearlong project.

Spencer and Rebecca enjoying the relaxed lifestyle by the sea.

CHAPTER 15

As we entered the house, almost exactly a month after the robbery, Rebecca walked straight over to the bathroom. The broken pieces of glass were still scattered over the floor. I stopped her at the door. She stood there quietly, staring out in front of her. I could see that she had some recollection of what had happened there.

"Dadda broke Mommy's house," she said, pointing at the broken window. Exactly how she had experienced and interpreted the events of that night, we couldn't be sure. She was barely two years of age. I knelt beside her. I was at a loss for words. I had absolutely no idea how to explain it to her. *At such a tender and innocent age, how do I tell her about all the bad things in this world?* She looked at me with her crystal blue eyes, so pure and still unaffected by all the evils that torment us.

"Daddy had to, my sweetheart. We had to get out of there quickly and we could not leave through the door."

She spent another few minutes staring out in front of her and then softly touched the scar on my forehead. Then, as if waking from a daydream, she left to go and play.

Spencer never spoke about it much. In most of his daily activities, he carried on as normal. He was still the same happy and bouncy child. He played outside in the garden all day and sat in the trees with the owls. The only discernible difference was his fear of the dark. He dragged his duvet, blanket and pillow to our room each night and slept on the floor next our bed. One day, while driving to school, he finally asked me about it. The drive to school was a 35-minute trip on the gravel road and another 20 minutes on the highway. This gave us plenty of time to talk about things.

"But why did that man do it?" he asked unexpectedly.

"What man?" I asked surprised.

"The bad man, with the big gun, who told me to give your laptop to him."

He only asked me about it that one time and never again brought up the subject.

Spencer is a thinker, an inherent quality he has inherited from both Brendan and me. I knew he was quietly thinking it all over in his head. There was just this one thing he hadn't understood.

The question caught me off guard.

"I don't know, my boy. People sometimes do bad things. Sometimes they have no choice and
sometimes they just don't know any better."

The truth is, I had no real answer; it was something I didn't quite understand myself.

By then, I had studied Psychology for four and a half years to try and understand human behaviour and I was still no closer to finding the answers I eagerly sought.

It is a moral issue and it is an issue of circumstance. It is an issue of culture and of norm. It is what that specific person finds acceptable or unacceptable within his own frame of reference and background. Because of the poverty and socioeconomic challenges in South Africa, most of us have accepted crime in our daily lives. We have readjusted our thinking and our attitudes about it.

I often hear people say, "They are only hungry." I don't mind if someone takes bread that does not belong to them. I can sympathise with a hungry person, stealing only to survive. It is the violence that comes with the crimes I cannot embrace. To some, violence is acceptable and even appropriate if you aim to achieve a resolution. People demand attention and change through violent protests and riots. Busses, trains and buildings are burnt to the ground whenever a group of people feels dissatisfied about one thing or another. This is a recurrent and standard practice in South Africa today. Or people turn to hate speech to express their opinion.

We have adopted a culture of violence. It is alarmingly common in the lives of ordinary people in our country. It is the plague of our time and, for the most part, we have given up the war against it. Rapes, killings and genocide have become a part of our sad human tale.

It is not death that I fear. I have often thought about leaving this cruel world behind. But not as a mother, not while my children still need me. I was given a purpose to protect them, to guide them and to support them. I'll fulfil this to the best of my capabilities. It is the moments before death that I fear the most. I do not want to die as a result of a senseless killing at the hands of a person with misdirected anger.

I have pondered about the cause of violence over many years. Some believe that aggression and violence is caused by genetic factors, that these ingrained urges of aggression are more strongly felt by certain groups of people. Others blame the media and our exposure to violence in our day-today living. Violence takes so many forms that it becomes difficult to comprehend. I believe that violence is sometimes just the absence of compassion. For the most part, hate, anger and resentment are all part of our historic inheritance, for which many of our forefathers are to blame. This all translates into savage brutality towards fellow human-beings.

We made rules to protect us on the farm. These, we believed, would keep us safe. By 5 o'clock, the doors had to be locked. There was to be no driving anywhere after dark. We always carried self-defence weapons at night. The kids knew to stay clear of the windows.

We soon became very accustomed to this conduct; in time, it seemed normal. It became second nature. The kids were young enough to adapt easily and they were unfazed by the strange behaviour. Gunshots were expected background noise.

I accepted this disquiet life. I made peace with it. I believed that if we were not playing victims, we would be equipped to protect ourselves. In time, life became enjoyable again. I never gave up hope of finding somewhere where we could be free from these rules. Free and unimpeded. I still longed for a life untrammelled by fear. But I would not let this constrain my joy by obsessing over it.

However hard I tried, I couldn't shake the feeling that I knew the guy who had attacked us in our home. His face was engraved in my memory. I thought about it almost every day. Recollections of him passing by me started popping up in my mind. The brief image flashing through my head was so clear, yet not perceptible enough to organise it in my thoughts. I could see him for seconds only. I had no doubt that it was a genuine memory. For that brief instant, I could revisit the actual moment in time as if taking a walk through my memory; everything about it was discernible and familiar. It was as clear as reality, but it was brief. With time, the memory became clearer: I was driving when I saw him, and so was he. He was in a white vehicle. In the same vision, I saw a fence and a big open field. And, just as suddenly, it was gone again.

I woke up one day from a dream about this very thing. It was like an itch underneath my skin that I could not satisfy, or scratch. I had to find a way to piece it together. For my own sanity.

Then, when I had almost stopped thinking about it completely, it suddenly dawned on me. I knew where I had seen him. I ran to Brendan. I was almost excited to exclaim that I was not losing my mind.

"He passed me on the farm road. That's where I saw him. He was in a white bakkie!"

"The security manager of the farm next to us drives up and down, along the fence, in a white bakkie," Brendan answers. "You must be thinking of him."

"That's the man who robbed us! It's the same guy; I'm sure of it!" I insist.

"You know it's nearly impossible to identify someone after such an attack; you've said this yourself," Brendan says, cynical about my
revelation. "But

I'm sure. I'm 100% sure. I knew I had seen him before when I stared him in the face that night and he knew it, too. It made him nervous, because he knew that I recognised him. The vivid flashes drove me almost insane, but now I know. Beyond reasonable doubt. That was the man," I answered.

"It just doesn't make any sense," Brendan replied.

Two months passed and then our donkeys, three Jennies, went missing. They wandered off the farm when the farm gate was left open by mistake, by one of the workers. They were rescued donkeys, adopted by Sam, the landlord Wayne's ex wife, who'd brought them to the farm. After she and Wayne got divorced, he wouldn't allow her back on his property, so she left them behind. Wayne didn't handle the divorce well. He suffered a breakdown and turned into a drunk. He lost complete interest in life and in the farm. We rarely ever saw or heard from him. We took it upon ourselves to take care of the abandoned farm animals which, besides the donkeys, also included three horses, four sheep, two pigs and a flock of geese.

By now, Brendan had forgotten about my cognizance of our attacker. He didn't give it much thought at all. He assumed that it was a way for me to deal with the matter - a form of selfempowerment over the sense of powerlessness induced by the situation.

After going on a long search, a neighbour informed us that our donkeys had last been spotted on The Farm (The Farm is known by another name, but for the security of my family, it will only be know as The Farm in this book). This was the farm directly on our border fence. The Farm is a public, state owned farm, enjoyed by many recreational users for a variety of outdoor activities, including mountain-biking and birding. A beautiful piece of landscape, it is managed by a committee of people, and an independent farm manager and security company are employed for daily operations. We drove over to meet with the farm manager to try and locate our missing donkeys.

The Farm Manager, Dave, receives us amiably. He is a well-spoken guy, who seems successful in his own right. He has a herd of cattle that grazes on the lush grassland of The Farm. The cattle are his own. This is an arrangement he has with the farm committee, to make use of the land. Brendan, in his usual friendly manner, strikes up a conversation with Dave, first about the cows and then about our work with the owls and a birdwatching event that we wanted to organise at The Farm. I nod and smile in all the right places. I quietly wish Brendan would just get on with it and ask about the donkeys, but he is too polite for this. He finally asks Dave if he would mind if we had a look around the farm to plan the bird-watching day we would like to organise for the members of the Rescue Centre, partly as a fund-raising effort for a new project we would like to take on, and partly as an awareness campaign for our work. Then he mentions the donkeys.

We are directed to follow the dirt road to a boom gate. Dave will radio Uuka, the head of security, to meet us there and take us to the bird-hides. He will also show us to the kraal to where they herded the donkeys.

Brendan slowly drives up to the boom. He rolls down his window to greet Uuka, while I lean forward to peek through the driver's window so that I can get a better view to greet him, too. As I lay eyes on him, I go stock-still. I immediately recognise him. I do not say a word, just gaze at him without blinking.

"Dave said that you would let us in so we can have a look at the community-centre and the bird-hides for an event we are putting together," Brendan explains.

"Yes, Dave said so. You can follow me," Uuka replies.

I dare not say anything that could place us in a troublesome predicament. I feel the same tightness in my chest that I get every time I am overcome with fear. *How strange is this situation? We are meeting, in a normal, disciplined fashion, with a guy who had a shotgun pointed at our heads just a short while ago.*

Brendan does not suspect anything yet. I don't want to risk our safety, so I keep completely silent. I don't even discuss it with Brendan, because this may change his approach.

We stop at the first bird-hide. Uuka gets out of his white bakkie and waits for us near the entrance of the hide. I avoid spending too much time in his company and stay back a bit.

Instead, I direct my attention towards the kids. I am careful not to act suspicious or nervous. He may pick up on any behaviour that is out of the ordinary.

Brendan explains that we have released about sixty owls in the last year.

"Many of them should take up habitat on Hills & Dales Farm. Therefore, hosting something here would be ideal. In fact, it would be perfect to make it an evening event so members can observe some of the owls," Brendan explains. With this, they start discussing the security factor. There is always some risk to hosting an evening event, especially in a rural area like this.

"Would you provide additional security, should we decide to invite our members here in the evening?" Brendan wants to know.

"That won't be a problem, but it will cost extra," Uuka responds.

"What is your security like here? Have you had any incidences?" Brendan asks curiously.

"We take care of it," Uuka answers conceitedly. "We have big guns. If we find someone, we shoot them and throw them in the river."

I can't believe the nonchalant confession. The country is lawless. Lawless and ruthless.

"What about the cops?" Brendan questions.

"What about them?" Uuka answers, with an overly-confident smirk. "They cannot trace these guns. Here, we look after ourselves," Uuka continues. "You have

Zimbabweans working for you. That is your problem. You must get rid of them."

"I trust my guys; they are good people. They have been working with me for a long time," Brendan responds, steering away from this topic of conversation.

"We have snakes!" I utter, without giving it any thought. My fear is now redirected into anger. I am incensed by his blatant arrogance. I so badly want to put him in his place. I want to warn him not to ever come near my family again. And threatening with snakes is the best I can come up with in the heat of the moment. As if possessed by my rage, I continue with the absurd lie: "We are animal behaviourists, so we know how to work with them. They are calm around us, but they will not allow anyone else near the house. This is our new security. It works very well."

I cannot believe the load of hogwash that has just came out of my mouth. I'm usually an honest person. I have gotten completely carried away. But he would have to prove me wrong. I know that he is not exactly going to sit and play with snakes to see if they can be tamed or trained.

"Eish, snakes, really?"

"Yes," I respond confidently, "Black Mambas, Spitting Cobras, Puff Adders, the whole lot."

He looks at me like one would look at someone who is completely deranged. He frowns, as if to think it over for a minute. Brendan interrupts with a question about the donkeys. Uuka displays an instant change that immediately reveals his innate brutal and callous mien. He is not happy that we are there to collect the donkeys. He has already suggested to Dave that they can be made to work on the farm. This is common practice in Africa.

"You are not taking them! Prove to me that they are yours!" he says in an intemperate outburst.

Brendan's posture is altered by Uuka's response. His shoulders pull back and his spine straightens in defence. He has just realised it, too - who Uuka really is. Brendan may not remember a person's face and he saw Uuka's face only for a very brief moment during the attack, but voices; now that is something Brendan does not forget! I heard him once taking a phone call from someone whom he'd met only but once, over four years prior, for whom he had installed an Owl House. He had immediately recognised the person's voice and Brendan had known exactly to whom he was speaking. He couldn't remember the man's name, but he could remember the exact address, he could describe the house and he remembered every bit of the conversation he'd had with the guy that day. For him, a voice triggers a memory cue that helps him to make the identification.

In this specific instance, his memory was prompted by Uuka's aggressive tone. He had used the same tone on the night he'd attacked us and given us orders.

Brendan cuts the conversation short. "You know they are not your donkeys and you know that I am missing three donkeys. There is no more proof required. I'll send my guys to fetch them." Brendan gets back into the driver's seat. The kids and I are already waiting in the car for him. For most of the drive home, Brendan is quiet. I can see by the expression on his face that he is conflicted by this predicament.

CHAPTER 16

"You realise it now, too, don't you?"

"The minute he raised his voice...! It was as clear as daylight. His voice is exactly... it is him!" Brendan drifts in his thoughts. He has a worried expression on his face.

"What are we going to do about it? Do we call the police? We can tell them about the weapons too - the collection of illegal firearms he blatantly bragged about!" I respond, fidgety.

"We can't."

"But we must, we can't let him get away with it!" I exclaim, disturbed by the fact that a criminal, a man who pointed a gun at my family... my little boy... gets to carry on with his normal business, while I have been through absolute hell. "It's not right; he has to pay for what he has done. What he is probably still doing. Who knows what else he is involved in."

"We cannot trust that our Justice System won't fail us. Should we give him up and should he get arrested, they won't be able to hold him for long, without releasing him back onto the streets. We don't have much on him, only our own conviction and his casual discussion about weapons. He will be out on bail before the weekend. And if he finds out that we were the ones who opened the case against him, he will take revenge. He knows where we live. We may be next to land up in the river," Brendan explains, concerned.

"So, that it is then. We allow our attacker to live as our neighbour and just pretend the whole thing didn't happen. And it didn't matter! I understand the whole 'love thy neighbour' thing, but this is absurd!" I remark, annoyed and angry.

"That's not what I'm saying. He will get what is coming to him. He risked the life of my family - I won't just let that go! Things could have played out very differently that night; it could have gone horribly wrong. He shot through the door of the compound the night when Peterson and Di came to us, so he obviously has no regard for life. But we cannot do anything about it right now. Not while we are still living here. Once we have moved away and there is no way for him to find us, then I'll make sure he gets what is due to him."

"I'll get on with it, then. Finding a place." I take out the laptop that was donated to us by an elderly lady who backs our cause and who'd read about the robbery. The support we've received from perfect strangers is what has kept me going. I switch on the laptop and immediately start searching for advertised farms. I look for somewhere even more remote than where we are now - somewhere away from Johannesburg. I want to be as far away from people as possible. While I am surfing through the property sites, my mind wanders back to Uuka.

I walk over to Brendan in the kitchen, where he is preparing food for the dogs: cooked rice and bone meal. I put my arms around his waist. I want all this to go away. All the bad feelings I have bottled up inside. Mostly the fear. He is taking it hard, too, but he knows that there is no room for weakness right now.

"People probably wouldn't believe us. He is a hired security-guard! He works for a well-known organisation; one that is feared by many." "They are known for taking the law into their own hands! And for them, law is whatever suits their own needs!"

"I spoke to Bryan," says Brendan, changing the subject. "He is considering moving into the cottage on the farm here. He's out of options. His lease is up where he is and the owner's brother is moving into Bryan's place at the end of the month. He's been given notice and is battling to find an affordable place. I already spoke to Wayne about it and negotiated a good rent for him."

We had met Bryan just over a year ago. We had been invited to set up an information stand for Owl Rescue Centre, in the animal park at the showgrounds in the South part of Johannesburg. Bryan had been doing daily bird and reptile presentations for the annual show event. After ten days of working together, we'd all become friends and had kept in contact afterwards.

"And Frank?" I want to know. Bryan had taken on Frank as his assistant after Frank had lost his job at the age of sixty-two and found himself in dire straits. His employer hadn't paid him for six months. Frank had lived in a small little rondavel on the same farm as Bryan, but had been evicted when he'd no longer been able to afford the rent. Bryan had offered Frank a place to stay and a meal each day. In return, Frank had helped to look after the birds and assisted with basic things in the show. Frank had a background in audiography, so he knew everything that there is to know about the sound equipment that Bryan used for his performances. Frank was not an animal person but, over time, he'd grown fond of all the critters. He was responsible and had played his part well. Frank had an unfortunate life story. He had faced judgement and scorn his entire life, because he'd been born with a cleft palate. In his later years, he developed a skin disorder from an infection in his nerve cells. It caused large red hives on his face and neck that were often puss-filled. The condition would flair up at certain times and welts the size of a 50c coin would appear on his face. Other parts of his skin would have flaky patches peeling off. His overall complexion was red, or even purple, from scaring. His curly, scraggly, bristly-textured ginger hair stood up wild and untamed on top of his head. People treated him like he was contaminated. Most just kept their distance. He looked like a homeless drunk, but he was neither.

Frank could smoke a packet of cigarettes a day, but he was not a drinker. Those who got to know Frank would learn that he was an intelligent, extremely well-read, gentle soul. He was an interesting character to talk to. His knowledge ranged over many subjects, from Psychology to World History. I spent many hours listening to

Frank's stories of his time in the army and in Rhodesia, before it became known as Zimbabwe. I often wondered if he'd been prevented from achieving success because of his outward appearance that society refused to overlook. He was deemed a social leper. Frank had a collection of prized possessions that he had bought and accumulated over the years - fancy sound equipment, tools, furniture, books and music, all perfectly looked after. Wherever he moved, he left nothing behind. His pride was retained by having these assets. I was worried that his stuff could get stolen. On the farm, nothing was safe. He was a sentimental person and kept letters, photos and medals from his dad and from his life as a young boy. He had never married, but had been wholeheartedly in love with a woman at the age of 19. Their paths had diverged when he'd come to South Africa, hoping to set up a better life for the two of them. Zimbabwe was in ruins. When he returned, he found that she had moved on with her life and was with another man. Her mother had told him that she was better off without him and that he should not pursue her. And he had believed her. He later heard from a family friend that she'd had a baby boy. By calculation of the age of the boy, she must have fallen pregnant during the same period that they had been together.

He'd always wondered whether the boy was his. He had lived a very solitary life from then onwards. The only other blood relative Frank had left was a brother who lived in England.

"Yes. Frank will come with. There are two rooms, so the place is ideal for them."

"Good."

The made-up story I'd told Uuka about the snakes was not so far-fetched now. Bryan had plenty of snakes. He was permitted to keep almost all species imaginable, from vipers to cobras. He'd had a passion for scaled creatures since he'd been a young boy. As an adult, he'd always been involved with animal training, education and conservation. Bryan and Frank moved in before the end of winter.

I made signs in all nine official South African languages and stuck them up all over the farm and everywhere around the house: "Qaphela inyoka!"; "Beware of snakes!"; "The owners of this farm will not take any responsibility for bites caused by
venomous snakes!"

In Africa, there are many strange, superstitious beliefs surrounding animals, but no animals are more greatly feared than snakes. They are associated with evil spirits and the power of their venom is feared even by those who do not carry the same superstitious beliefs. I made sure that Bryan did the necessary displaying of his African Python, the largest of his collection, all along the fence line. It was only necessary for one person to spot the enormous snake to initiate the 'bush telegraph' that would spread the news far and wide. Information like this travels like a veld fire in rural areas. It may sound like an irrational concept, but we didn't have many other options left that would keep trespassers away. I wanted to send a clear message that we would no longer tolerate the farm raids. It seemed to work, at least for a while. I enjoyed the companionship of Bryan and Frank on the farm; it gave me peace of mind that others were close by to help, should we ever need it. We also became good friends with some of our neighbours, Jan and Conal, both bachelors, who grew up in the area. Finding a woman to suit their lifestyle was an immense challenge for attaining a wife, so both had remained single. Conal was a chicken farmer, who lived right next door to us. Everyone in the area bought their farm fresh eggs from him.

We became acquainted with Jan through Conal, but our friendship with Jan became meaningful after one late night when he came to help us where we had broken down by the river. We were returning from a visit to my parents, when the Musso's wheel fell off. The wheel-bearing broke loose from the driveshaft and the left front of the Musso literally fell flat, with its nose resting on the tyre - a very distressing situation on a dark night. Shortly after we broke down, three suspicious men came walking towards the car. They changed their course when they saw us and started wandering in our direction, like vultures changing their course of flight upon seeing a carcass. A patrolling securityvehicle spotted them at the same time we did. The security officer kindly offered to wait with us, as he, too, could see that the men were up to no good. (This is how opportunistic criminals have become.) The kids were asleep in the back of the car and I was sitting inside the car, with a crossbow resting on my lap. Jan's house was about four kilometres away. Brendan needed a wheel spanner to temporarily fix the problem and Jan was bringing one. It would help enough at least for us to get home. Jan kindly came out at this ungodly hour and spent another two hours following us home, with the wheel coming loose every 100 metres. We would stop and the two men would have to get out, lie flat on the muddy, dirt road to put it back on. I made coffee as soon as we got home.

Jan stayed, sharing intimate details about his life, until well after midnight. He had been married before and had a little girl of his own, but he'd only known his ex-wife for six months before they had tied the knot. She'd fallen pregnant shortly after that. When things had started going wrong in their relationship, the once presumed love between them had turned into hatred. (Someone once told me that there is a thin line between love and hate, but I never understood this term until years later when I observed how divorced spouses so often mistreat and turn on each other.) Jan's ex-wife, in pure bitterness, had fabricated a claim of molestation against him and he'd been restricted from visiting his daughter - a battle he had fought in Court for four years. All evidence pointed in his favour, as there were no signs of abuse; however, the courts tend to be biased towards the mother, and so the case was dragged out over many years. His wife later remarried, had another baby with her new husband and lost interest the daughter. Today, Jan has full custody.

Jan sat on our couch, recounting his story. It was like he needed to get it all out. The words came out of his mouth like the eruption of that science experiment you do when you add vinegar to baking soda to create a volcano. And that was how a life-long friendship was established. That was how things were on the farm. We were a close-knit community, who greatly depended on one another. This was probably the only good thing that ever came out of the crimes that had been committed - the bonds that were formed among neighbours. We were fighting alongside one another in what felt like a battle in a senseless, undeclared war. In cities people live within metres of one another, but hardly know one another by name. On the farms, where murders were becoming a daily event, a connection between neighbours was a necessity for survival. I was the only woman among a band of men. This meant that dinner and get-togethers were almost always at our place; I was the only one who could cook well enough. Brendan built a lapa and firepit, where we enjoyed many nights socialising outside, under the open skies, like normal people do. Armed, but normal. We had potjiekos at least once a week, prepared outside over the coals, in a large, round-bellied, cast-iron pot, with three disproportionately short legs. We were happy once more. I started drawing and painting again. You can always tell my mental state by my expression of creativity. When I'm happy and content, the paint and brushes come out. I would sit outside, in the shade of the big, hundred-yearold wild-fig tree, drawing pictures of the owls and capturing time with brightly-coloured paint. We planted a vegetable garden and I grew herbs in large wooden crates, all around the outside of the house. Gardening was my therapeutic escape to wonderland. I planted sage, thyme, rosemary, basil... all the culinary herbs I could find. No meal was prepared without them. We invited Frank and Bryan over for dinner most nights. The entertainment industry wasn't exactly booming and the two of them had a tough time scraping money together. I made sure that they ate a decent meal at least a few nights each week. Bryan's shows are phenomenal. He is probably the most talented person I have ever met when it comes to performance. He was born to stand on a stage. But people are overstimulated in today's world, nothing 'wows' us anymore. People weren't exactly lining up to book Bryan for a show. Even the schools had become too busy to spare 45 minutes for an educational animal show. Kids see far greater things on satellite television, he was told. Bryan and Frank's cottage was about twohundred metres away from our house, past the cow kraal and a short walk towards the pedestrian gate that Brendan had made from palette wood and bamboo.

Bryan loved the animals on the farm, all but one. And if there was one thing Frank hated more than the 'night walkers', as we now referred to the criminals who snuck around at night, it was a sheep we named Satan. The enormous black sheep hadn't always been known as Satan; this was a suitably beastly moniker that we'd given this ram after he had become vicious. Satan used to be the friendly one among the sheep we had on the farm.
He would often come up to where we were sitting, for attention or even a head tickle. One day, over the Christmas season, some men had come along and stolen his wife, a beautiful Swartkoppersie ewe, whose body was lily-white and head as black as coal. He had been left to look after their little lamb on his own. From that day on, he'd

hated all men. Whenever he saw a man, his eyes would turn red and stiff and he would charge headlong into the male foe, launching his attack at full speed, with his crown forward. His mass and strength could severely injure, or even kill, if he managed to hit his target in a certain way. Fortunately, he didn't exercise the same hatred towards me or the kids; his beef was with men.

Bryan refused to admit his fear of this monstrous animal. He would tell stories about how he had trained bears and wrestled with lions in his younger years when he'd worked on movie sets. Compared to a bear, how intimidating can a sheep be? Sometimes, though, when Bryan took an inordinately long time on his walk over for dinner, we would catch him hiding behind a tree. When Satan was anywhere in sight, Bryan would quickly dive to take shelter behind the nearest tree or shrub. With his gut pulled in tight, only the orange tip and smoke of his cigarette would be visible. It caused us great amusement and we never let him live this down. Bryan and Frank both suffered under Satan. Frank once arrived at our house, full of cuts and lesions. Satan had apparently launched him into a rocky garden. Brendan, however, refused to be bullied by a sheep. When Satan came charging, Brendan stood waiting, feet apart, knees slightly bent - the same position you would adopt in a rugby match, when preparing to tackle your opponent. Then, when Satan was close enough, Brendan would grab his two front legs and twist him to the ground. He would hold him down long enough to intimidate him. An animal who has lost its fear of humans always turns into a problem and can be very dangerous. Brendan believed that he needed to reinstall this fear in him. It would be the best thing for everyone. "It's either this, or he will end up as lamb chops very soon!" On some occasions, Brendan, would go so far as to hop onto Satan's back when he came charging, as if to break him in. He would hang on for dear life, like a bull rider, while Satan bolted towards the river. I couldn't contain my laughter as I stood watching. Satan would do his best to unseat Brendan, but eventually he would run out of energy and just stop. Brendan would get off and both would walk away as if nothing had happened.

Over time, Satan recognised what would happen every time he charged Brendan. However, this was a devious sheep, with a soul as dark as his coat. He waited for opportunities to present themselves. One day, Brendan was on the phone with a new volunteer named Jo-Anne, who was coming to help at an educational event we had planned for the next day. He was standing by the owl enclosures, with his back turned to Satan, not paying any attention to the evil sheep's presence. Satan stood watching for a long time, glaring at Brendan out the corner of his one eye. Brendan was deep in conversation when Satan took his chance. He rammed into Brendan with all his might, launching him off his feet. Brendan landed up in a mud puddle, while his phone went flying in another direction. Jo-Anne was still on the line, able to listen to the furore that was about to go down. Satan was about to set off his second attack when Brendan rushed to his feet. Enraged by Satan's deceitful actions, Brendan tackled the 120kilogram ram and forced him to the ground. He held him down, with his right arm in a firm grip around the ram's neck. He balled his left hand into a fist so tight that his knuckles turned white. Then he punched Satan repeatedly, while cursing in anger. That day Brendan took out all his accumulated rage and frustration for every underhanded thug who had ever wronged him, on the sheep he had pinned to the ground. [Brendan believes in a fight with an honour code, even between enemies. Instead, we were in a war where nothing was fair. Every night was an unruly battle with unlawfulness]. When both were completely exhausted by their combat, Brendan slowly relcased his grip and Satan ran off. Brendan picked up his phone and continued his discussion with JoAnne. She seemed a bit dumbfounded by what she had overheard. That was the last time that Satan ever troubled Brendan. He had taught him a lesson that even a sheep was intelligent enough to learn.

CHAPTER 17

Brendan cleaned up the old chicken run and repaired the chicken mesh, to make it safe from predators. He had an idea to start farming with chickens. He had done some research and had realised that there was great earning potential in the industry. We needed to devise a plan to supplement our income. We were earning some money from manufacturing and installing Owl Houses and some from renting out rat traps, but none was enough to sustain our living conditions and still grow the Centre. We could get 1-day-old chickens for free-ranging at a very good price, and he thought that it would be a good idea to farm with them for food for the owls and to sell the surplus. Brendan spent days cleaning, disinfecting, painting and repairing. He installed heat lamps, food trays and a water source.

When it was finally ready, we received a call from a lady who had raised banded mongooses and needed a new home for them. Katinka, a sweet lady with a soft spot for animals, had bought two of them as pets and had hand-raised them since they'd been babies. The pair had grown up and had had four offspring of their own. The whole lot had been hand-raised by Katinka's family, in their family home. After some time, though, they had become increasingly aggressive and Katinka's husband could no longer go anywhere near the male mongoose anymore. The kids also had been bitten on occasion. They had become a problem, like all hand-reared wildlife eventually do. Katinka had had no other choice but to lock them up in a parrot cage she'd had in the garage. However, she'd realised that that was no life for them. She'd heard about the work that we did with the owls and insisted that we were the right people to help her to reintroduce the band of mongooses back into the wild. We had done this successfully with hundreds of owls, but we'd had no experience with mongooses. Katinka was afraid that if she took them anywhere else, that they would end up being sold into a zoo somewhere. She didn't want that for them. She realised the mistake that she had made by buying them as pets and wanted the right thing for them now. She loved them like we all love our furry friends; they had been like a cat or a dog in her house, until they no longer were.

We felt compelled to help. We would apply the same principle to this release as we did with the owls. They need a space where they can become accustomed to the area first and where they are fed and can establish a territory. After a view weeks, we would open up the enclosure for them to leave on their own terms. They would know that they could return for food anytime they needed to and that it was an area of safety. Eventually, they would be able to wander into the nature reserve and find their own territory. This was the plan, at least. This meant that our project with the chickens had to wait. We didn't have any other suitable place to keep the Banded Mongooses and the chicken run was ideal. Katinka, accompanied by her entire family, including her mother of ninetytwo, came to bid farewell to the little creatures that had crawled deep into their hearts. The old lady walked with us as we gave them a tour of the farm and showed them where the mongooses would be kept during their release-preparation period. Katinka was fighting back the tears as the time came when she had to let them go. I felt honourbound to care for them as best as we possibly could.

The mongooses were fascinating creatures. Similar in appearance to meerkats, they moved fast and were very agile. They were very sociable little creatures and vocally expressed themselves in different situations. We fed them some of the same things as the owls, but allowed them to scavenge for their own meals, too. They dug up worms and insects and ate some roots and plant matter. We were pleased when they learned skills that they would need in the wild. We broke human contact and interaction with them as much as possible, hoping that they would unlearn their imprinted ways.

After about 6 weeks in the run, we thought that they were ready to go out into the world. There was a small hatch towards the bottom of the chicken run that we left open for them to wander through when they felt ready. We stayed back and only observed from a distance. Once they left the chicken run, they became very inquisitive about their surroundings. There was a clear region around the chicken run to which the mongooses kept. You could almost draw imaginary borderlines that they would not cross over. Their actions were perfectly coordinated. The big male, the father of the brood, was in charge and they all followed his lead in absolute synchrony. With a chattering sound, the whole group would come to a standstill, heed and obey. A slight change in this chatter would signify danger that would choreograph a unified attack. The same chattering noises, followed by hissing sounds, were used when they hunted. We once watched them gangup against a Snouted Cobra. The cobra stood up in a hood to warn them off, but the mongooses pursued, escaping each of the cobra's deadly strikes. With fleet-footed movements, they sprang out of his way. With rapid and energetic jumps, they pranced around their victim, each in turn grabbing onto a part of the snake. It didn't stand a chance.

One day, for a reason unknown to us, the dominant male led them out of their normal area and down towards the river, towards Neil's house. The band returned a day later, but the male leader was nowhere to be seen. We assumed that he had been eaten by a jackal. There was a den with a jackal family not far from there. Due to their domestic background, they had no fear of big predators. They had been raised around dogs and didn't understand the danger. They would easily fall prey to a hungry predator. Once the ruling male was no longer around, their behaviour changed. They were without guidance or direction and behaved like a bunch of rebellion teenagers. There was no longer a clear territory within which they stayed, nor did they stick to the normal foraging routine that they had followed every day. They wandered closer and closer towards our house and became curious about us and our actions. Before long, they made themselves comfortable on our furniture and all over our living space. With the prepatent male gone, they didn't portray the same aggressive behaviour either. Our efforts to release them into their own natural environment failed, but they could integrate into our family without any trouble.

Every so often, we would give them each a whole uncooked egg. It was hugely entertaining to watch them crack it open. It would result in an eggtossing game. When they saw an egg, they would break out into an excited chorus of high-pitched chitter. They would all scuffle to get their hands on it. Once they got hold of the egg, they would run with it to a rock or wall, scurry into position about half a metre away from the rock, facing the opposite direction, with a stooped stance. Legs spread apart, they would get ready. Just as a footballer snaps back a ball, so the mongoose would fling the egg back between its legs against the hard surface to crack it open. Eventually, they completely moved away from the chicken run; instead, they would sneak into the house, just before dark, and crawl up into Spencer's bed. They would make themselves comfortable under his duvet, giggling like schoolgirls. When Spencer got into bed, they would hiss and shrill. He didn't mind them one bit. They would move over and share the bed with him. Spencer had a big Kingsize bed, with enough space for him and the gang. He is very tolerant of all animals and sees them as equal to him. He wouldn't dare chase them out.
This is where they slept every night.

With the chicken run free, Brendan could start up his project. It earned us enough money to create a nest egg for future plans. We hadn't given up on our dream of finding a place that was unassailable. Brendan aspired to buy a property for Owl Rescue Centre. He wanted to purchase, rather than rent, a piece of land for the owls - a sanctuary where they would be protected and looked after, a piece of habitat that would always belong to them.

Kobus, an estate agent in the Hartbeespoort Dam area, had a property to show us, just outside the border of Gauteng. The property was located on the old road that we used to take to Sun City, before they built the new highway, along the Magalies Mountain Range. I used to travel that road at least once a year with my parents, when I was younger, on our trips to the Pilanesberg. It carries a nostalgic memory of a childhood filled with dreams and hopes. It winds through a breathtaking mountainous landscape. I always look back with fond memories of those vacations at the game reserve. I have always been a bit of a "bush baby" and am happiest when I am outside in nature. I never tire of spotting animals in the wild.
I get that same excited feeling as I used to get on Christmas, when Mom unpacked the presents under the tree. Each animal has a charm that enraptures me, from the smallest of birds to the impressive Big Five - they all hold equal merit.

Our appointment with Kobus is at three o'clock. Ben, with his son Lukas, drives up towards the house in his double-cab bakkie, fitted with a bull bar, nudge bar and cattle rails on the back - serious autochthonous farmers, those two. Their family farm had been passed on from many generations before. Ben is in his fifties, not yet at retirement age. Lukas is 18. They are dressed in typical farmer's attire, khaki-coloured shorts, khaki button-up shirts, and leather lace-up shoes. Both are sturdily-built men. Lukas is the spitting image of his dad and one would assume that he would naturally follow in his dad's footsteps. You would expect him to take over the running of the farm when his dad hit mid-sixties, but he has different ambitions. He knows everything about harvesting a good crop and cattle management. He grew up with his toes in the soil and playing in fields among the cows. But he would tell you that things are different now and that farming is not as appealing as it used to be for young men in this country. Instead, he is being groomed to play rugby one day for an overseas club. They came to purchase a thousand chickens from us, not for commercial use but, rather, for a self-subsistence project for their farm workers. An admirable undertaking.

"It's a beautiful piece of land you have here," Ben says, while turning and walking away from the chicken run to face the impressive natural scenery that overlooks the Jukskei River.

"Yes," Brendan answers, "we are just renting here, but it's quite something. If it wasn't for the crime, we would probably have bought a piece of land and lived here forever. We are meeting with an estate agent later today about another property. Hopefully, we will buy there."

"It will be sad to leave here," I add, "but our safety will always be at stake, if we stay."

"You've had problems here, then? Bloody bastards! What area are you looking at?"

"It's out there near Hartbeespoort, just off the R104 on the way to Mooinooi, as I understand it," Brendan answers.

"You must be careful of that area, too. I know a few farmers out there. As long as it is well before Majakaneng. The farmers there have a hard time," Ben warns. Ben's farm is also in the North West, but towards Thabazimbi. "I'll phone Kobus and check with him, before we go all the way out there for nothing. If there is any risk of the same issues there, I'm not interested."

Ben and Lukas have barely said goodbye when I get Kobus on the line. I've been looking forward to this day for a long time and Ben's words have left me feeling very discouraged. Kobus assures me that the property in question is in a peaceful area and there is absolutely no likelihood of anything happening, like what we'd experienced in Hills & Dales.

Kobus is parked on the side of the main road, at the entrance of a gravel road, in his white Mercedes Benz SUV, waiting for us. He is obese and looks awkward behind the wheel. Brendan pulls in next to him. He greets us through his car window and explains that the property is about three kilometres up the dirt road. The road to the property is rocky and bumpy. He shows us a vacant piece of land, with beautiful valleys and a mountain backdrop. Kobus battles the section of uphill climbing towards the midpoint of the property. We climb onto a rock, from where we can survey the whole open space. The land is positioned in divine nothingness. Only age-old trees and lush green vegetation. It would be owl heaven. A perfect sanctuary. There is an immemorial farmhouse, broken down right down to its foundation.

"Does the property have a borehole?" Brendan asks, interested.

"No," Kobus responds. "No borehole and no electricity."

The property is breathtaking, but unattainable at this point. There is no way that we could afford the bond to purchase the property, the cost of building a home and a sanctuary, and still worry about a borehole for water and laying electricity cables. I'm not sure what we were thinking. We were thinking well beyond our means.

"We need this, but with a lot more. We need a place with some existing infrastructure, even if it requires a lot of renovation. We can improve on it over time, but we aren't in a position to build up something from nothing. We don't have the resources for that," I explain.

"It may be a bit much to ask and an unrealistic expectation." Brendan was the one who taught me about dreaming big and about finding ways around the obstacles. There is always a way, if you are willing to persist long enough. The world is a big place. We don't have to stop looking for a better life right here.

"I may know of another property," Kobus suddenly remarks, as if he's just had an epiphany. "The bush lodge next door is for sale; Roger has been looking for a buyer for over five years now. He may be interested in considering a 'deed of sale' proposal. I can talk to him about it if you want and get back to you."

Brendan and I had spoken to Roger about his property about two years before. I'd found his advert on one of my Internet searches. He hadn't been interested in our offer then, but people's circumstances change all the time. He might look at it differently now.

"Is his place still on the market?" Brendan responds. "It would be great if you would."

Brendan and I had stayed at Roger's bush lodge a few years before, on our way back from an owl project. Spencer had been only a toddler back then. He had crawled around in the dirt and played with Roger's dog. I had liked its rustic appeal. It was a modest and informal place. The TV lounge had looked like a room in an old person's house, with ball-and-claw furniture and leopard printed cushions. We'd watched the Springbok rugby game there. It was the bushveld surroundings that drew me in. It reminded me of my childhood fantasies, where I had role-played in the character of Sheena. The bush is where I most felt that I belonged. I was queen there and at peace with the world. We had revisited the place, after I'd spotted the advert. It had been a bit rundown and dilapidated. He had closed the doors on it three years before and had left it for the earth to reclaim. It certainly had potential. With some hard work, it could be fantastic. It had accommodation for guests, it had a dormitory for school camps, a house for us and our staff, and enough space to develop the Centre into anything we wanted. The structures were all built from natural, raw materials, like wood and stone. Exactly the way I preferred it. A building should not detract from the beauty of Mother Earth.

On the way home, the lodge was all I could think about. This was our one chance. We had to make it work. We discussed ways of acquiring the money to pay for it. Ideas we could compile in the presentation that we would present to Roger. One idea was to sign up members of Owl Rescue Centre. We could offer the public the opportunity to become more involved in our work, I thought. We would have proper premises where people could come and visit, see what we do and even stay over. I was so excited, that I immediately started to research ways to set up easy fundraising tactics. We would host school camps, and volunteers from all over the world could book to stay with us and share in our experience of working with the owls. We've often had interested parties contact us; this was our opportunity to grow to a new level. If all else failed, we would open the lodge to public visitors for overnighting.

When Kobus phoned back, he had explained how Roger had lost complete interest in the place and was open to our proposal. To Roger the property had become nothing but a white elephant. I could not believe that my dream could be someone else's nightmare. It was only the following year that I would understand the irony inherent in this thought. Roger agreed to meet with us on the 9th of September - a day before my 31st birthday. If things turned out well in the meeting, I would have good reason to celebrate. I would have accomplished one of my life-time objectives - to own a piece of bushveld.

When I was thirteen, I convinced my dad to buy a property in Marloth Park. We vacationed in one of the luxury lodges in Malelane and visited friends who had a house inside the park. It bordered the Kruger National Park and enjoyed visits from the same wildlife. My dad cleverly saw it as a good investment opportunity, while I believed that he had bought it for us to enjoy summer holidays there. He sold the property a year later, without my knowledge, and made himself a quick couple of grand. I was crushed when I found out about the sale. My dad is a businessman; I should have been smart enough to realise that.

The opportunity had me exhilarated and anxious at the same time. It felt like I had four winning numbers on a lotto ticket and only needed two more to make all my dreams come true. I had my mind set on a new beginning somewhere else, away from the bad associations of the farm. I dreaded the day another bad experience would happen. I was so fixated on this that I could not bear the idea that Roger might not accept our offer.

We all sat down at a large round boardroom table in Kobus' office. Kobus had invited Lindell, a conveyancing lawyer, to join us in our discussions. Lindell doesn't look like a typical lawyer. She had a soft and feminine appearance, her demeanor was easygoing and relaxed. She was someone I could relate to. I immediately felt at ease in her presence. I was relieved that she was not the usual uptight and pompous kind of professional who uses fancy jargon to assert her intellectual ability.

Brendan had a quick chit-chat session with Roger, before we went into the formal discussion. He leaned his body towards Roger and sneaked in the question, with a 'no-bullshit' attitude: "Are you interested in this agreement? Would this work for you?" Brendan is a simple, honest guy. He believes in a gentlemen's agreement. Your word is your bond, kind of thing. He was not interested in the legal stuff; he left that up to me. As long as there was a clear understanding between the parties involved, a handshake agreement was all he needed.

"Yes, otherwise I would not be sitting here," Roger remarked.

Kobus formally introduced everyone. He ordered us each a cup of coffee. I have read that this makes people more agreeable in a meeting (drinking coffee). Something to do with the caffeine and the reaction it causes in our brain. I wonder if he knew this trick too. I opened the conversation by explaining our whole situation - the robberies, our challenges and so forth. I was an open book. I didn't want pity from any of them, nor did I want Roger to agree to it unless he felt that he could benefit from the agreement as much as what we would. I wanted final reassurance that we were making the right decision. It would give us the confidence to go ahead. It was a big, bold step to take. It was something that could potentially ruin us financially. We were investing our life savings in the deposit and taking on a project that was unfamiliar territory to either one of us. It was not like anything in which we'd ever been involved before. The monthly instalment on the Deed of Sale agreement was R100 000, which meant that we had to generate a monthly turnover of at least R150 000 to pull it off, not to mention the hard work we would put in to restore the place before we could do anything with it. There was also the cost of the erection of all the aviaries to consider. If we slipped up just once, the property would transfer back to Roger and we would lose everything that we had put into it. However, all this would still be worth it if we could secure the safety of our family. The well-known psychologist Abraham Maslow described security in his Hierarchy of Needs as one of the most basic of all human needs, second in importance only to breathing, hunger or thirst. This is because without it, from living in incessant fear, one would eventually lose one's mind, if not one's life. They all seemed shocked by our dreadful story. Roger had assured me that he had never had any issues with crime, nothing to speak of, or even worth mentioning. Kobus concurred and emphasised the statement by referring to his own experience as an agent in the area. Kobus continued to explain that he had lived most of his life in the area and could guarantee that it would be a good move for us. (We later learned from staff who used to be in Roger's employment when he still operated the lodge, that

this was all a falsity. Roger himself was robbed at gunpoint in the house that would be ours - a deception staged for desperate and credulous buyers.) Brendan and I had a solid plan to pay for the property. We would sign up members for the cause that would require them to pay a monthly membership fee. I approached a financial institution, which set up a debit-order system for us. This would allow us to collect monthly debits, with their signed permission, from the cause supporters' accounts. The public would have the opportunity to become more involved in the cause, attend releases of owls and even stay over at the lodge when they felt like taking a break from the city. I was brimming with excitement and enthusiasm. Other income would be generated from volunteers scouted from all over the world, who would be willing to travel to South Africa and pay for the opportunity to work with a variety of owl species. I compiled a brochure with activities they could look forward to, like a five-hour hike to observe the Cape Vultures at the top of the Magaliesberg Mountain. Bryan and Frank would move with us and we would each have our own distinctive roles to play to make it a success. Bryan would present his bird shows and teach the volunteers more about snakes, with reptile presentations. The balance of costs would be covered by our other projects. Our owl houses sold well and peopled were excited to find a solution for rodent control that is harmless to the environment. The chicken sales were also increasing. We were in a charmed position.
Things were looking up for us.

Roger agreed to sign a six-month lease, at an appreciably lower rate than the monthly instalment that would be due, once the contract had been converted to the Deed of Sale in April of 2015. We would have six months to set it all up and grow the earning potential to exceed R150 000 per month. It was a calculated uncertainty and gamble to sign the contract. When one's family is threatened and the onus of your children's' existence and happiness lies heavy on your heart, there is no impediment too great to overcome. I am not a risk taker, but the desperate desire to achieve something led to my unpresuming oversight of human weakness. In the end, each person favours his or her own personal interest above any other. This was something I would learn when it was already too late.

CHAPTER 18

We moved in during the hot summer of the year 2014. Our contract commenced on the 1st of November. We had our work cut out for us. The move was the first obstacle to overcome. We had a house-full of furniture, personal belongings and a multitude of animals to move - four dogs, a cat, two mongooses, three donkeys, five pigs and sixtyfive owls. It was utter chaos. I proclaimed that it would be the last time that we would relocate. "This is home now," I said to the kids. "We don't have to be frightened anymore. We are a far distance away from the baddies." Roger's assistant, who still lived on the property, handed me a bunch of keys. He explained that there was a bucket in the office that contained the rest. This was as far as his help extended. One needed the skills of Sherlock Holmes to solve the puzzle of which key served what purpose. Kerry-Lynn arrived in the middle of the disordered mess of scattered furniture and marked boxes. Brendan had met Kerry at the Bird Park a few months earlier. She was a contract worker, studying towards a qualification in Nature Conservation. The bird park informed her that they wouldn't be renewing her contract and she was looking for a job. Brendan got word of this and invited her to meet with me for an interview. It was easy to see that she was the right person for the job. I had an important exam coming up - the final module before receiving my qualification. My mind was as scattered as the boxes, with divided attention on different responsibilities. I didn't feel worried. The fulfilment I received and complacency I felt when building towards the life we had dreamt about, had placed me on a euphoric high. I felt invincible and as if I could take on anything. Spencer and Rebecca were running around barefoot along the red-sanded pathways, with eager excitement, adventurously exploring their new surroundings. They were experiencing a new kind of freedom. I relaxed my usual guardianship, which allowed them spontaneous movement around the farm. For the first time, I felt safe enough to let go. Hindered only by the occasional thorn from broken, weather-beaten thorn bushes covering the sand and stone trails, they uncovered each stone, each footprint, bush and tree in the wide open spaces of their new, bushveld home. Exploring the unique variety of ruined timbered-, stone-and-canvas dispersed constructions, the hills, the trees and the mountain, was like finding myself lost inside wonderland. We'd had very little knowledge about the property when we'd signed the agreement; in fact, we'd known only two things: it was safe and it was ideal for the owls. I felt the same excitement as a child opening a gift that she had quietly wished for. In the midst of unpacking and moving boxes, I followed a pathway up to one of the highest- positioned tents that had a panoramic view of the mountain range. There, I paused for a minute to take it all in. I took a deep breath, as if to inhale the beauty that surrounded me. In that, though, was also a nervous gasp that I could also lose it one day. However, I knew to appreciate it entirely in that very moment and for as long as what I could. There, with my feet planted firmly on the harsh, torrid ground, I made a promise to myself. I promised that I would never tire of the splendour of my whereabouts. I would never look up at the mountain and not appreciate it for its magnificence. I had found myself in a place I previously could only dream about. I could not believe our luck. As the hours went by, the sky turned bright red and orange in colour - like flames dancing on the horizon. The sun was setting over the dusty planes of the bushveld land. Brendan made a fire for us and we all gathered around it to warm from the crisp, cool, night-time air. It was a moonless night and the stars were particularly bright, shimmering through the treetops in heaven above us. Brendan, Frank, Bryan, Kerry and I celebrated our first night together in our new dwelling. It would signify the start of a venturesome journey that lay before us.

CHAPTER 19

Building a pool was Brendan's first major task and priority. We decided that we would open the lodge to the public in the interim, before signing up enough members and volunteers to cover our expenses. This was only meant to be for a short period. A temporary solution. A pool was something that the lodge could not do without. We were amazed that Roger had managed to run the place for five years without one. The diurnal temperature was excessive and, at mid-day, easily exceeded forty degrees Celsius. The seasonal rain showers were late that year. We needed a good downpour. Everything was covered by a dusty coat. The earth was baked dry, scattered with shrivelled leaves, thorns and bushes. The heat of the sun reflected off the red sand; it felt like a scorching furnace beneath my feet.

Within eight weeks, the pool was complete. Brendan designed and constructed it above the ground, partly to avoid any accidental drownings of small wildlife, and partly because it was easier and took less effort to build. He used double utility bricks and steel reinforcement to strengthen the walls and framework. We all had our reservations as to whether the structure would be able to withstand the pressure of a hundred thousand litres of water. The project consumed our last bit of savings; however, it was an investment with a promising return. We would be able to advertise the lodge, with a beautifully large, sparkling pool, an oasis in the centre of a bone-dry bushveld landscape.

We stood in anticipation and watched as the water rushed in. Brendan smirked in triumph. The pool filled to the top, with the walls still solid and in place. "Not even a leak. How could you have doubted me?" Brendan gloated. He likes to be praised, to get an occasional pat on the back.

I obliged. "I don't know why I ever doubted your engineering prowess. You are a genius," I responded with a ludic smile.

By December, the lodge was filling up with guests. I felt like a fish out of water. My intrinsic introverted personality usually shies away from people and yet there I was, playing hostess to a diversity of visitors from all different walks of life. The ones I could relate to, with similar viewpoints and interests to my own, were easy to accommodate. The other unreasonable, bloodyminded and ill-bred individuals, however, were a bother. I always acted politely and was respectful, regardless of the person or situation, even while grinding my teeth unseen and reminding myself of the bigger picture.

On one occasion, Brendan had to ask a family of four to leave the lodge after the wife had screamed and shouted at me, using the most unladylike language over the most trivial things - there was not enough wood packed, to her liking, to keep their bonfire going, and a light around the braai area needed to be replaced. I stood stupefied, while she insulted me. Frank, overhearing her rude tone of condescension, was so nervous that he broke the lightbulb in his hand. She then turned to him and remarked on his incompetence. I had stood quietly when she'd acted offensively and abusively towards me, but my necessity to protect others would not allow Frank - an elderly man who had suffered under people's mistreatment his entire life - to become the object of her scorn. In the most diplomatic manner possible, I told her what I thought about her unacceptable behaviour. But my tender character was unversed in this unsophisticated, boorish, verbal brawl. Brendan stepped in and asked them politely to leave. They overnighted in our lodge and checked out early the next morning. Her husband, while handing me the keys, apologised to me for his wife's bad behaviour, while she sat waiting in the car. He said that they were newly married and he was still unsure of how to handle her at times. He explained about the difficult time she'd been through a month before and the stress that she had been under and told us that she felt remorseful over the whole thing. I accepted the apology for his sake. I pitied him, though, as I've never believed in an excuse significant enough to justify that kind of conduct. He wished me luck with our endeavour, to which I responded: "And good luck to you, too." I could not begin to imagine what it was going to be like for him to have to live with someone like that every day for the rest of his life.

On another occasion, a lady named Sharon booked into one of our bush tents with her boyfriend and two sons. A veld fire had broken out on the mountain a few hours earlier and a red line was barely visible on the tip of its highest peak.

At about 10 o'clock that night, Sharon phones in a panic: "Hello, is this the owner of the lodge?" Brendan answers, rising swiftly to an upright sitting position: "Yes, yes, it is, how can I help?"

"Did you see that there is a fire on the mountain?"

"Yes, we're aware of it. We've been keeping an eye on it. You don't have to worry; it's no threat to us now. It's kilometres away."

She hangs up, dissatisfied with Brendan's incautious response. Half-an-hour later, the phone rings again. The same number. This time, Brendan gives the phone to me to answer.

"Hello, Danelle speaking."

"I want you to go and put out the fire immediately! This is ridiculous!" Sharon utters confrontationally, without even a greeting, or introduction.

"I promise you that there is nothing to be concerned about. We have spotters keeping an eye on the fire. It's very far away," I respond.

"You cannot expect people to sleep like this. I don't understand why you refuse to do anything about it? Why don't you just put out the fire?"

"Sharon, I appreciate your concern, but I hike these mountains often but tonight is not going to be one of those times. To reach the fire would take approximately five hours, if we moved briskly. There is no other way to reach it, but by foot. Even if I managed to make it up there in the darkness and in time to make a difference, I doubt I'd be able to extinguish the fire."

Sharon, now beside herself with anxiety and enraged by our response to her distress, hangs up the phone.

Just before midnight, she phones back. I pick up. There is heavy breathing on the other end. "I can't stay here. I'm asthmatic, there is too much dust. I'm having an attack. Will someone please come here and refund me. I'm packing my things and leaving this very minute."

On a weeknight, a few weeks after we had opened the lodge, I was busy preparing supper in the industrial-type kitchen of the lodge when a strange man came bursting through the kitchen door. This was usually a quiet time at the lodge as we hardly ever had guests during the week. Kerry and Bryan were both in the kitchen with me. Brendan was with the kids.

Spencer and Rebecca were running around in their PJ's fetching twigs and pieces of wood to make a bonfire.

"I can't believe it! There is actually some activity going on here!" roared the words of the uppity man blocking the doorway. He was a stout thirtysomething guy, cocksure and lordly - a guest, or at least a potential guest, I assumed.

"Can I help you?" I asked, surprised and a bit defensive, ready to give an excuse as to why there wasn't someone waiting in Reception. We didn't expect anyone to book in. We hadn't received an inquiry for this night.

"And who are you?" came the pompous response.

"I am....well...." I feel a bit like Alice having to answer that. His forward manner had made me twitchy and a bit uptight. "Who are you, I should ask? You are standing in my kitchen, so it
shouldn't matter who I am. Who are you?"

"Well, if this is your kitchen, then I'm your neighbour," he replied, as he took a step forward, with a smile playing on his face, and extended his right hand to shake mine. "Martin. Pleased to meet you. Welcome to the area."

He then proceeded to introduce himself to Kerry and Bryan. I was left feeling sheepish for my complete misunderstanding of the situation. I invited him to have coffee with us and we joined Brendan and the kids at the fire.

That was my first impression of Martin. The weekend after that, he brought his family to meet us - wife and kids, his dad, mom, two of his three brothers and his one brother's wife. His parents reminded me of an old-school staunch

Afrikaans couple. They looked like they had just fallen off an ox-wagon. His mother's long grey hair, that could reach all the way to her bottom, was tied tightly into a large bun on the top of her head and she was dressed in a dull, old-fashioned frock. His dad wore a dull, brownish-yellow coloured shirt and pants pulled up to his chest. He reminded me of a bullfrog. These two episodes illustrate the kind of person Martin is - a people's person, with a large network of acquaintances he refers to as friends, he's very much a hail-fellow-well-met kind of guy. From being at first a stranger barging through one's kitchen door, followed thereafter by an introduction to his entire family and then being invited to dinner in their family home, all within a short while, he certainly made a fascinating first impression!

Martin and his wife later became very good friends of ours. Gwyneth is probably one of my closest and dearest friends today. What I first perceived as arrogance in Martin, I later realised was boldness, gregariousness and self-confidence - characteristics of a sheer extrovert. Gwyneth is slightly more reserved, nurturing, warm, kindhearted, loyal and wise beyond her years - an old soul. She's the kind of friend anyone would wish for.

Brendan's mom came to stay with us for three weeks in December of that year, to help me with the kids. We had moved into one of the bigger wood cabins, one without a working bathroom, for the first few months, to be closer to the lodge and our guests. Our house was another one-and-a-half kilometres higher up on the property, towards the mountain, which was rather inconvenient when having to attend to guests' needs at odd times of the day and night. My mother-in-law used the chalet directly opposite from ours. This had felt rather adventurous, at first. It had been like a permanent camping escapade, but the situation had grown increasingly uncomfortable over time and I'd found myself longing for a family home. To cook, for example, I had to wander down to the communal lodge kitchen. To shower, we had to trek up to the ablution facilities, where bush showers were heated with a fire under a drum that is called a 'donkey'. It was too warm to wear closed shoes with socks, and our feet became stained red-brown by the sand. Despite the heat, I later changed to permanently wearing my hiking boots to safeguard my feet that had gone from pedicured to cracked, dry and soil-marked. Regardless of the heat, the small cabin and awkward lifestyle, I still felt lucky to live in an environment made up of thorn trees, grassland and wildlife. To have so much beauty around me was wondrous. I accepted these things as a unique part of the African bush; it was a setting that I know I will romanticise about my entire life. As much as I griped over these conditions, I loved how alive it made me feel to live where we did. It provided a way of life that was thrilling and exciting. I gained a strange sense of fulfilment from being pushed beyond my normal, refined comfort zone. Within the quietude of nature, I felt fulfilled.

Between the guests, the owls, the kids, the projects and my part-time studies towards my degree in Applied Psychology, our days were long and tiring. We were up with the sun and only got to bed late each night. Our schedule changed to a seven-day-a-week one, with our weekends taken up by other people's needs.

Late one Sunday night, a lady phoned to seek help with an owl she had come to 'own', that she'd bought from a man standing outside a police station. He had stood there wanting to sell her a box of five Barn Owls but, at a cost of R500 each, she had only been able to afford to buy one of the owls. Excitedly, she took her new pet home. It hadn't taken long for her to realise that she had made a horrible mistake. Brendan answered the call. He asked her a few of the normal important questions to check on the owl's well-being. "Did you give the owl anything to eat?"

"Yes" she answered, "I gave it bird seed, but realised that it didn't like it very much, so I googled what I should feed it. The Internet
mentioned mice, so I went out and bought it one."

Brendan informed her that an owl needed more than one mouse per night and that she should give it at least three during the course of the night, at four-hourly intervals. He said that we would only be able come out there on Wednesday to collect the owl.

"This is starting to cost me a lot of money," she replied. She had bought the mouse for R10 and was displeased to hear that she would need to spend four times as much to properly care for it over the next few days.

Later, the phone rang again: "I'm actually very upset with this owl now; it smells very bad and it ate my parakeet!" she exclaimed.

Brendan, baffled by the lady's ignorance, asks her how this had happened.

"I had nowhere to put it, so I thought it could share the cage with my parakeet," she answered. "Only the parakeet's feet were left when I checked the cage! I have spent the last three years teaching that bird to talk," she continued in a vexed tone.

Brendan couldn't help himself and broke into an inappropriate, but brief chuckle.

"It's not funny!" she responded angrily. She had become desperate to get rid of the owl. "I let it fly freely around in my house in the hopes that it would go, but it won't leave! The damn thing won't leave!"

Again, Brendan battled to contain his laughter. She then asked if we would refund her the R500 that she'd paid for the owl when we collected it from her on Wednesday. Brendan replied that we couldn't do that. We hadn't sold her the owl, but still she expected us to refund her for it. By purchasing the owl, she had contributed to the illegal wildlife trade, which annoyed Brendan. She was a fool and would have to pay her own school fees.

The lodge was growing in popularity. I had to block out days on our calendar over Christmas so that we could spend time with the family. Brendan's brother Stuart, and his wife Ann, came over for Christmas Eve dinner and spent the night and Christmas day with us. Stuart had towed a big trailer loaded with the two quad bikes that Brendan had arranged to buy from him over a few instalments. I hadn't been on a quad bike since primary school when my sister's boyfriend at the time, Francois, had taken me for rides around their farm and attempted to teach me how to ride by myself. As I jumped on the back with Brendan and we raced up to the foot of the mountain, I felt like I'd been teleported back to that carefree time in my life. I set the table, carved from the trunk of an enormous tree, in colours of red, silver and green. Flickering flames from candles and paraffin lamps provided soft light on the rustic wood deck, fringed with tree branches and the crowning leaves of a large Marula tree.

Bryan dressed up as Father Christmas to entertain the kids. Rebecca helped me to carry a plate of cookies and a glass of milk to the round wooden table at the bottom of the stairs. I gave Bryan a little bell to ring when he came strolling through.
This was meant to get Spencer and Rebecca's attention. Worried that they might recognise Bryan, I told them to sit quietly and watch from the top step of the staircase. I convinced them that we might scare off Father Christmas if we tried to approach him. He carried a black bag over his shoulder, took a bite into one of the cookies and chased it down with a sip of milk. Then, in his typical showman

style, he bellowed a loud "Ho ho ho" and walked off. The kids were thrilled, eyes bright and sparkly, in complete awe about what they had seen. To this day, Rebecca still talks about that one time that she saw Father Christmas. We waited five minutes to give Bryan time to change back into his normal clothes, then followed into the lounge, where the Christmas tree stood. I had snuck in earlier to stack the gifts under the tree. We exchanged gifts amongst ourselves and with Bryan, Kerry and Frank, whom we now regarded as an extension of our family.

CHAPTER 20

The farm had five Zebra, eight golden Wildebeest and nine Impala inhabiting its thorny, dry earth. The Wildebeest, golden in colour, is considered royal game and is worth almost half the total value of the farm. In our agreement, Roger had clearly stated that the Wildebeest were not part of the sale and that he was in the process of finding a suitable buyer. The Wildebeest would remain on the farm until such time. It was breeding season. The dominant male was trying to establish his territory with loud grunts and peculiar behaviour. This often turned into an aggressive charge to chase away anything or anyone that he perceived as a possible threat. The animals were all relatively familiar and used to people, which meant that they were not afraid to saunter in close proximity to the lodge. It was not unusual for the animals to stampede through the boma, chased by a hostile, brawny beast. We would have to run, grab the kids and dive for cover.

It was February, the silly season was over and fewer visitors were booking into the lodge. The air was sweet with ripe marula fruit. Timothy, Bryan's son, and his girlfriend Kikki, came to visit for a few days. A Red-chested cuckoo, or Piet-myvrou, the Afrikaans name by which I'd known it as a child, was singing all day and well into the night, in loud vocal calls. In old Afrikaans folklore, we were told that the Piet-my-vrou's first calls meant that it was time to put on your raincoat. We were hopeful that soon the clouds would burst open in a shower and soak the dry earth.

We created a large bonfire. Mesmerised by the flickering flames, we sat enfolded by darkness and the shimmering stars above our heads. I looked up and remembered when I was younger and had wished on falling stars. I believed with all my heart that they would one day come true and now I believed they did. I had all I could hope for. Rebecca was captivated by the croaking frogs. Spencer and Rebecca, each armed with a flashlight that they'd received from Nikki in their Christmasstocking, went looking to find every single toad they could. When she found them, Rebecca would, in one smooth swoop, grab two or three frogs at a time and hold them in her hands. She would giggle excitedly and come running in delight to reveal her treasure to us, before releasing them to hop along on their merry way.

Tim suggested that we go looking for scorpions. He had brought along an ultraviolet light, which makes scorpions glow in a vibrant blue-green luminous colour that stands out against the dark background of the night sky. It sounded like an interesting activity for the kids, so we all agreed. Brendan, Bryan and Frank stayed behind, while the rest of us strolled along on our little adventure. I lagged behind the group, carrying Rebecca in my arms, stumbling on the rocks and uneven ground underfoot. The only light we carried with us was the small, ultraviolet flashlight. Tim pointed out rocky areas where we would be most likely to see scorpions. As nocturnal predators, they would be active now.

We had made it just past the cottage, walking up towards the mountain, when we heard a rustle in the nearby bushes. It was coming from the dense brushwood area, a few metres ahead of us. We stopped to listen and when we thought it was nothing to worry about, we proceeded on our way. The herd of impala was startled and ran off and disappeared into the night. Then we saw it. Lit up under the moonlight, it stood glowing-white - an enormous, muscly, ghostly beast - and emitting chilling groans. It seemed larger in appearance than the animals I identified during the day-time on the farm. "A buffalo... or bull.... what it that thing?" Kiki yelled out in alarm. We had upset the animal with our intrusion. He stamped forcefully on the ground with his right forepaw, churning up a cloud of dust around him as he grunted, huffed and vigorously blew air through his nostrils. For a moment, I stood dead still, overwhelmed by the vision of this powerful creature.

"Run!" yelled Tim. I could suddenly feel the adrenaline pumping through my veins. I ran, with Rebecca still clinging onto my hip, to the nearest tree. We got separated from the rest of the group and a dirt road separated us from Kiki, Tim, Kerry and Spencer. I wanted my little boy with me, but I didn't dare to cross the road at that point.

"Spencer, are you okay?" I yelled out in a panic.

"Mommy, I'm scared!"

"I'm coming, don't worry, I'm coming!"

I knew that Tim and them would look after
Spencer, but I preferred to be there to protect him myself. I
was about to dash over the road, when I heard heavy
stomping on the ground.

"Stay where you are!" shouted Tim.

I stood as close as possible to the trunk of a tree, with
Rebecca slightly pushed into the stem and branches. The
animal won't run into a tree, so this is our best chance of
safety, I thought to myself. It was dark all around, with the
trees blocking out any moonlight. I had no idea on which
side of the tree to stand, nor from which direction the
animal would charge. I could hear Spencer's sobs just a
few metres away. That's it, I'm going to take the chance
and dart across the road to Spencer. I managed to meet up
with the group and with Spencer.

"I want my daddy!" Rebecca cried. She knew that in times
like this it would be better to have Brendan around, rather
than me. Kiki had her phone with her. I whispered to her
to call him to fetch us in the bakkie. We were sitting low in
the grass, surrounded by a couple of thorn trees, each of us
staying very alert to the surrounding activity, peaking over
our shoulders in all directions.

A few minutes later, Brendan and Bryan were there to pick
us up. The Wildebeest had disappeared and was nowhere
to be seen. He had vanished as if he'd been just a part of
our imagination. Later, we giggled about the whole ordeal.
The fear we had felt in that moment when we'd seen the

Wildebeest was a different kind of fear than the fear I'd experienced when I was being threatened by a thug with a gun. In a strange, indescribable way, it had been an enjoyable fear - one that had made us feel alive. We had felt a rush of excitement and adventure. Where the other kind of fear had left us miserable and depressed, this one had us laughing when recalling the scene. The difference, I suppose, lies in the intention of the act. The animal felt threatened by our presence and reacted only to warn us off. However, when people come to rob, their intentions are depraved and wicked. The act is antagonistic and personal, therefore I am still left emotionally marred because of it.

A few weeks later the Wildebeest were all sold. In time, a Zebra named Zoey became interested and tame towards me, although Brendan was afraid of her. He claimed that she didn't like men. Around me, though, she was gentle. Whenever she spotted me, she would walk up to me to be stroked and then follow me for a while, before breaking off to return to her herd. I enjoyed our bond and her company.

The Centre became busy and we had owls pouring in from all over. The rains came and when there were enough insects around, we planned our first big release of the juvenile Spotted Eagle Owls that had come in during the breeding season. It was all a great success and I couldn't have been happier.

As a pro-life Centre, we do everything in our power to save every owl that finds its way to us. In some cases, the owl sustained injuries that caused irreversible damage, which makes it unfit to return to the wild. Our philosophy here is that if an owl wants to live, let it live. In other words, if it is determined that the owl can still have qualityof-life, despite the injury, it is placed in one of our habitat aviaries where it can live freely in a controlled environment. These permanent residents of the sanctuary are used as foster parents in our baby owl rearing program. One such special owl is Hedwig, whom is a blind Spotted Eagle Owl. Once the Spotted Eagle Owl babies are a couple of weeks old, we place them with her. The eagerness in her when she hears the feeding call of a new arrival is exceptional to observe. She immediately tucks them in underneath her wings and starts the feeding and rearing process. Archie and Betty are two Giant Eagle Owls, or verreaux's eagle-owls as they are now known (the biggest owl species in Southern Africa) whom have each had one wing amputated. They live in a large openroof habitat enclosure on the Sanctuary and we've built them a big nest using a tractor tire. We are hoping that they would breed; we would release their babies back into the wild. During breeding season, our bedroom is stacked with brood boxes with nestling owlets of various species and, using tweezers I would feed freshly cut rat meat to the hungry gaping mouths in bi-hourly sessions throughout the day and night. This is an immensely satisfying task, nurturing a helpless little being and watching them as they burgeon and progress as if right in front of your eyes. It is a job I selfishly keep to myself and don't allow our staff to do, partly because I don't trust another with this important responsibility but mostly because it brings me fulfilment unlike anything else. After a few months, with only short breaks in between it does take its toll on me and I feel like a sleep deprived mother of a new-born baby that refuses to grow up. I have watched as hatching owlets wiggle and slowly break their way out of an egg and watched as the same owl takes it first flight into freedom. This experience is something I couldn't possibly describe in words.

Brendan constructed a wood platform in a large Marula tree, leading up with a staircase from our upper deck of our double-storey cottage, where he installed our bath. In the same tree, a Barn Owl house was installed and used for some of our releases and is now permanently occupied by a Barn Owl family. We sit nights in the bath watching as the daddy Barn Owl hunts for his family in clear sight of us. There is always much excitement from the babies inside as he drops the prey in. And within seconds, he is off again hunting for the next meal. We use these large constructed Owl Houses to release unfledged Barn Owl babies that come into the Centre. The house is completely enclosed, except for an entrance hole at the front with a landing platform, or veranda as we like to refer to it. I would raise and nurture the babies up until they are old enough to eat on their own. When they can swallow their food whole, I know that they are ready to go into a release Owl House to prepare for their journey back to the wild and it is time for me to break contact with them. It is important to Brendan and me that the owls don't imprint on us, to ensure that they have the best shot at surviving in the wild. The babies are always released in groups, usually about four to eight owlets are placed inside a Release Owl House at a time. Once they are in the Owl House, they no longer see us feeding them and the food is simply placed inside the house and on feeding platforms around the release spot. When these owls develop and become curious and adventurous, they will one by one pop their heads into the hole to look outside and observe their surrounding environment. They soon become habituated to the area and once their flight feathers are grown, they start taking short flights to the nearby branches of the tree. They stay there for a while before returning to the safety of the Owl House. After a few nights of the same routine, they finally work up the courage to wander further and soon they are hunting on their own. We monitor their hunting behaviour by checking the pellets they regurgitate – as soon as we see the bones and fur in the pellets changing from day-old chickens (which we commonly feed when we do a release for this very purpose) into the remains of rats, mice and other natural prey, we reassured that they are coping and we can slowly wean them off our support. They return to the Owl House before sunrise every night and spend their days in the comfort of its interior. The owls slowly adjust to the wild and their survival rate is equivalent to that of parent-raised owls. We spend a lot of time on the release process and view it as an intricate part of our success with the owls. Most of the owls that come to us, are released within the protected area of the Sanctuary. When they are ready, they move off and find their own territories. When there are too many for release or there are species that may require different habitat, such as the Marsh Owls, we seek out game reserves and natural areas, faraway from human interference where we would erect a temporary release hack for the same 'softrelease' process. We would camp out in the reserve first, checking for prey availability and other owl species, that will make it a fit area. There are twelve different owl species within South Africa, but we most commonly rescue the ones that have become known as urban owl species, namely Barn Owls, Spotted Eagle Owls and to a lesser extend March Owls. The usual four rescue cases a month soon turned into twenty cases a month, which again changed in more recent times to sometimes over a hundred cases a month.

Our Sanctuary is now the largest Owl Sanctuary of its kind in the world. Owls can be observed visiting the various feeding platforms around The Sanctuary, every single night. Many have taken up residency in the Owl Houses where they breed year after year.

CHAPTER 21

In April, everything changed. Our six-month grace period was up and our monthly instalment went up to a hundred thousand Rand per month. We could pay the first instalment with money that had been left to us in an Estate. The donor was a stranger to us and we only knew her by the name the Executor of the Estate used when referring to her - "The late Mrs. Zita Coetzee." She had left R150 000 in her Will to be used for owl conservation. With the funds, we could secure a sanctuary for the owls, where they would be protected and looked after, a piece of habitat that would always belong to them. I wrote to the Executor of her Estate and asked to be put in touch with her family, as I felt the need to thank someone. I wanted them to visit and see first-hand what we did for the owls. Mostly, I felt that I should do something in the honour of the deceased, who'd obviously cared a great deal about our cause. A simple and short note came back saying: "I'm afraid the deceased did not really have any close family." It deeply saddened me that she'd had no one in this world, that someone could be that alone. It made me grateful for everything that I have. I often thought about her, even though I knew nothing about her. I pretended that she smiled down from heaven with every rehabilitated owl that found its freedom again.

For a couple of nights, with an interval of one night in-between, I woke in excruciating pain exactly one hour after going to bed. Like a biological clock that activated a bomb, it would strike at an exact calculated time. The sudden stabbing pain behind my left eye would wake me screaming in agony. The pain, so intense that I felt like slamming my head into the rock wall to make it stop, would occur without any warning. It felt like someone was drilling into the nerves of my eye and through my skull. Inhumane, indescribable torture. Like a child, I would rock back and forth on the edge of the bed, tugging at my hair, with tears streaming down my cheeks, defencelessly defeated by my own body. Then, after about fifteen minutes of anguish, the pain would disappear. My sister's friend, Nicky, who is a doctor, suggested that I have an MRI scan done. Although she didn't say it, I feared the worst, that the pain could be caused by a tumour in my brain. I later discovered that it wasn't anything lifethreatening, like cancer. I suffered from cluster headaches, a condition described by some as the "worst pain known to medical science." The attacks only ever happened at night.

One windy night I was awake after another cluster episode, when I heard a faint calling at our door. The wind was tugging at the canvas that covered the netted windows and I had to concentrate to hear who was there. In a daze, I heard Kerry's voice. Brendan got up and opened the door, while I searched for a jersey to put over my nightdress.

"We've been robbed," Kerry said, calm and expressionless, followed by an unseemly titter. "They took my laptop right from under my bed. Bryan's, too. From there, they went into the lounge."

Kerry, a loudly vigorous woman in her late twenties, was not easily distressed. She tended to suppress her emotional needs, with only occasional bursts of atypical expressions of her own sentiments. Kerry's mother had battled depression and given up the fight when Kerry was a young girl. The trauma of watching an emotionally unstable parent - and then losing that parent to mental disease - had given rise to Kerry's restraint over her personal feelings. The idea of a brigand sneaking into your room and fiddling by your bedside while you lay asleep would terrify and deeply disturb most people, but Kerry remained unfazed. The news hit me like a speeding bus. Disillusioned, I lumbered towards the lounge, which was located directly underneath Kerry's and Bryan's place. I met Frank on the way there, who pointed out that the kitchen also had been broken into, but only a few steak knives were missing. The lounge had been left in a stinking mess. The kists, left to me by my late-grandmother, were open and the contents lay tossed out on the floor. It was 3am before the cops arrived. I had sat waiting, wearied by distress, on the coffee table with my legs folded and my head collapsed in my hands. Frank had offered to make a list of the missing items: 2 x laptops, 4 x speakers, projector, amplifier, toolkit, decoder, wireless microphone... and my flash drive with the first copy of my book. This single incident is not what caused our downhearted spirit - we knew that they would return. Up to that moment, we had lived with a false sense of security. This signified the start of a new battle of nights facing atrocity.

CHAPTER 22

During the bleak winter of 2015, we had seventeen robberies on the farm, which excluded the attempted thievery where Brendan or one of the guys managed to deter or chase after perpetrators and succeeded in foiling their intentions. On an early Sunday morning in June, while blackening darkness still fills the skies, I am awakened by a woman's scream, and think it's from a nightmare I was having. It had been a single screech, followed by ominous silence. I lie motionless, keeping my mind focused on what I think I'd heard – or had I been dreaming it?

A few minutes pass and then Frank knocks and calls outside our cabin door. "Wake up, wake up!" he shouts. "A couple has been robbed!" The sobs of a woman can be heard in the background.

Brendan jumps to his feet and swings open the door, wearing nothing but jocks. Her sobbing becomes more intense, almost hysterical.

"They took everything from us, even my ID and my wedding ring!" she ululates, while wiping her tears with shaking hands.

"Give me a minute," Brendan says and shuts the door to get dressed. He hurriedly makes his way over to them. I look over to where the kids are still peacefully and obliviously asleep in their beds, before joining Brendan and the couple.

The woman and her husband are guests in one of the tents that are less than twenty metres away from our cabin. Her name is Alina and her husband is John. Both are in their late twenties. They were recently married and had just bought a townhouse in the South of Johannesburg. Alina is a secretary at a financial company and John is a freelance graphic designer. Alina had woken up when a dark figure had emerged from the dimness inside their tented room and had stood, revealed by the moonlight, watching her from the edge of her bed. She had yelled out in fear, which had woken her husband who had been in a deep sleep in the single bed next to her. The man had rapidly moved in-between the two beds and pressed a knife against Alina's throat. Another man, wearing a beanie on his head, had entered the tent. "If you make a sound, we will kill you! Slit your throats and watch you bleed out like goats!" the vile man had forewarned them, in a rough dialect.

Frank, who had heard Alina cry out, had strolled up the pathway from his cottage in the direction from where he'd recognised the sound had come from. Three of the dogs had accompanied him, barking in the direction of Alina and John's tent. The anxious, hardened criminals had moved quickly, grabbing Alina and John's bags and their phones, and had forced Alina's wedding ring from her finger, threatening to cut off her finger, using the razor-sharp knife, if she showed any resistance. Minutes later they had vanished, blending into the blackness of the night.

I sit consoling the pair, while the sky fills with hues of purple, pink and orange. Brendan fetches clothes and shoes from his cupboard to give to John, who's been left with only the long johns he's been wearing. I try not to make my own upset state of mind visible to Alina and John. A small part within me even envies them for being able to leave, while we have to stay behind in this godforsaken place. I can offer little consolation; my own thoughts are racing with my own suppressed memories, so I leave to make us all tea, instead. John and Alina stay for another ten minutes or so, sipping their tea in silence, and then leave to go home.

Brendan, Bryan and Frank spend the rest of the day tracing footprints and repairing weak spots in the fence. The fence has been cut in different spots every time; separate entrance and exit holes have been made every time the farm has been invaded.

There was little chance of sleep during the long, cold nights of winter. I would lie awake for most of the passing hours and, even when I managed to fall asleep, I would wake in a completely conscious and alert state from just the slightest sound - trees blowing in the wind, rustling twigs, or faint crackling of leaves. One night, muffled voices, in the otherwise absolute nocturnal silence, has me sitting upright, wide-eyed and attentive. Before my hand can even reach Brendan's arm to wake him, his eyes shoot open, wide and bewildered. He quietly gets out of bed, fumbles around searching for his clothes, pressing his hands down on objects in the dark, feeling his way around. He puts on his pants and secures the firearm in the holster attached to his belt, then throws a dark, inconspicuous hooded-top on over his T-shirt for camouflage. Lastly, he sits back down on the bed and slips his feet into shoes, without wasting time with socks. Careful not to make a sound, he quietly opens the cabin door. The six dogs, who sleep in the cabin with us every night, all storm out the door at the same time, heading in the direction of the swimming pool. I await Brendan's return, jittery but prepared to defend myself while he is out, with a baseball bat in hand. My head rests on the wooden wall of the cabin. It is two in the morning; I'm dead on my feet. Brendan turns the corner near the big Marula tree and notices two men in the pathway between the wood cabins and the pool.

"What are you doing there?" Brendan shouts. The dogs are going mad, forming a battlefront between Brendan and the men. Without the slightest hesitation, the man, in silhouette, lifts his right arm and fires three shots in Brendan's direction. Brendan draws his firearm and returns fire. The loud thunderous cracks of gunfire echo against the mountain. *P-taff, p-taff, p-taff.*

The dogs scatter in different directions. Terrified by the loud bangs, they search for shelter. I quiver in fear. A crushing pain in my chest weakens me.
I want to scream. I want to cry. I want to throw up. Far in the distance, the shrieks of Barn Owls resound like ghouls calling to wake the dead.

Minutes later, Brendan returns with five of the dogs. It feels like I'm taking my first breath since the gunfire. The criminals have run off, toward the top of the property, and Brendan assumes that they ducked out through the fence.

"Where's Rocky?" I ask concerned.

"He must have run off when the shots were fired. I'll go find him." Brendan leaves again to look for Rocky, a small Jack Russel-cross that Jan had given us when his dogs had had a litter of puppies.

Two weeks before, Rocky had led a chase after four intruders. He had cut through a corner of a neighbour's property, and their two big dogs - a Bullmastiff and a Staffordshire bull terrier - had gotten hold of him, in turn. That he survived and escaped the jaws of the two ferocious dogs was nothing short of a miracle. When Rocky had returned to me at the cabin that night, he'd had a six-centimetre-long cut on his neck and we'd had to rush him off to the vet for stitches. He is small but incredibly brave. Brendan returns without Rocky. He is nowhere to be found. Minutes later, we hear Rocky barking in the distance. It is far away, but the sound travels in the silence of the night. Brendan goes out again to go find him. He is sitting at the top edge of the property border, at the foot of the mountain, barking into the darkness. He is facing the fence. Brendan knows that his bark can mean only one thing – there is someone out there, but it is off our property, so he calls Rocky and returns to bed. The next morning, Rebecca calls me excitedly.

"Mommy, Mommy come here, I want to show you something!" she exclaims.

"What is it, I ask," expecting to find another frog or lizard that has aroused her curiosity.

"No, Mommy, up there!" she says pointing into the sky.
"The vultures, look how many there are!
What are they all doing up there?"

I tilt my head up towards the clear blue skies, speckled with large-winged birds. Approximately three hundred gracefully soaring Cape vultures are circling just beyond our fence line, at the top peak of the farm. It is near the spot where Rocky had sat barking. "Come and see this!" I shout to Brendan.

His face turns pale as he stands there confounded, looking up at the watchful circling vultures. Brendan goes searching to see what they had been circling over, but can't find anything. It must have been nothing more than a mysterious coincidence.

CHAPTER 23

With each new sunrise, the remembrance of the night before was wiped clear from my mind. The days were filled with sunshine and happiness. We spent them hiking through the mountain range, along the riverine and through the gorge, looking for evidence of breeding Cape Eagle Owls. It was not that I didn't care about what had happened, but my first effort to cope and instinct of survival was to suppress any reminder or impression of our violent and hostile environment. I never associated day-time as a threat and therefore could spend it in oblivion to the danger that lurked in the dark nights ahead. The thing that I then tried so hard to achieve, was the very thing that would become so bothersome to me in the preceding months. I pretended that our circumstances were normal, when to do so was anything but rational. We became desensitised to the violence. Over time, we slowly became conditioned to it. Our frequent exposure to break-ins, robberies and gunfire every single night had weakened our awareness as to the severity of the circumstances. Our social acceptance of the violent conditions was altered. My harsh outlook on life and death became so far removed from who I used to be that I could hardly recognise myself in the words I spoke and thoughts I expressed.

We once sat around the table in the boma discussing ideas of how to capture the thieves and the things we could do to them. We would send a clear message, we decided, one harsh enough that from then on we would be left in peace. It would aid to take back control of our lives by instilling fear in our enemies, instead of the converse. We would no longer be victims, but make victims of the savages who oppressed us night after night after night. It was only talk, but my unrelenting thoughts scared me.

On a busy night at the lodge, slightly after 6pm, a message is received that we were going to be under attack later that evening. Often warnings came in the form of strange markings, signs or objects left behind by criminals at the location of a marked target. This was a form of communication between conspiring gangs. Some of the farmers became familiar with and knowledgeable on this symbolic language and could warn the community of what was transpiring. The signs were often inconspicuous objects that looked like rubbish, or a pile of stones. An upside-down tin can placed on the fence could mean that there was a vulnerable woman on the property, two red tin cans an indication that the owner was armed. A white object would mean that the house was an easy target, and if there was a blue object, it meant that there would be help from the inside. A pile of stones meant that there were dogs guarding the property, but two big rocks placed together would tell the criminals in cahoots that there were old people living alone on the farm.

On a quad bike ride late one Sunday afternoon, just before sunset, following the gravel road up towards a peak on the mountain, we noticed one of these signs placed in a tree. Rebecca was with Brendan on his quad bike and Spencer was holding on around my waist at the back of mine. This was the day that I discovered my inner strength, my fortitude in the face of adversity. On the left-hand side of the road, I noticed a white, plastic bag tied onto the fence of a neighbour's farm. The plastic bag meant 'easy target'. I didn't think anything of it at first, until I looked to my right and noticed four suspicious-looking men kneeling in a dried-up watercourse alongside the road, slightly concealed by grass and brushwood. There was no doubt that these were shady characters. They glared at us with hollow, wicked eyes, like sly, greedy hyenas. We drove another two-hundred metres and then stopped. Brendan was going to turn back to question the men about their intentions. He was about to hand Rebecca over to me when I turned and noticed that the men were approaching us, walking side by side along the sand road, with stones and half-bricks in their hands. We had ridden to where the gravel road ended. We could only return the same way that we had come in. Brendan warned me not to stall the quad. I hadn't been riding for long and to kick-start the twostroke bike was a challenge for me, even on a good day. It would take me a few kicks to get it fired up. I took a deep breath and followed closely behind Brendan. We climbed over hills and through thick bush, on a sloping stretch of ravine.

"The bike is your only weapon," Brendan exclaimed. "Use it! Don't stop riding. When they come for you, don't slow down. Drive with full force into them."

We turned the bikes towards the exit, in the direction of the approaching thugs. All I could think of was bricks and stones flying at our heads. I remembered a story I'd once read about a little child who had been hit by a brick, when his parents had landed up on a road where protestors had been launching rocks and bricks on cars passing by. The brick had shattered the back window of the car and hit the child in his car-chair.

The little boy had never recovered.

I mentally prepared myself to take them on. "They have stones. They will try and hit you off. Drive and don't stop. You can do this!"

In the meantime, Brendan had gotten hold of Frank on the farm. "Get your firearm and drive up in the bakkie! We need an escort out of here!" he'd explained to Frank on the phone.

Minutes later the red bakkie arrived at high speed. Frank was driving and Kerry was in the passenger seat next to him. We swiftly loaded the kids into the back seat of the double-cab Nissan bakkie and instructed them to lie flat.

"Get them out of here!" Brendan gave the command. Brendan and I stuck close, following the bakkie at full throttle back to the farm. We had managed to escape the ordeal unscathed, but I was worried that our luck would one day run out.

On the night that we had received the warning, it had come from a trusted member of the farming community who had been sent a message of caution from an informant within the squatter camp, where those criminals resided. The informants were the few good Samaritans who were silent activists against farm murders and what some described as genocidal attacks. The men of the agricultural community were all meeting within the hour at the most central farm, about seven kilometres away from ours. It was a warm, moonless night and I was busy preparing dinner for twenty-two guests when Brendan left to attend the gathering. The kids were hiding under the concrete-cast worktable until Brendan's return. Brendan was last to arrive at the old, rundown farm, where thirty men had congregated in the paved driveway, each holding a shotgun in one hand and a flashlight in the other. They were dressed in similar khaki-coloured clothing, almost like a uniform that is worn by the common farmer. An area map was neatly laid out on the ground, with the men crouched in a circle around it.

Brendan was the only one who was not braced for combat and was without a shotgun. He was also the only Englishman amongst the group of Afrikaners. Brendan and Neil had had their feuds in the past. One was over a proposed electric fence that Neil wanted to erect in the highlysensitive conservation area within the Magaliesprotected district. Brendan's concern was for the biodiversity of the area, the sensitive, semiendemic botany of the area and the restrictions it would place on the natural behaviour of the indigenous wildlife. The area was inhabited by a troop of sixty baboons that would be cut off from their water supply and the leopards would also be adversely affected. Neil argued that the purpose of the fence was for security.

On this occasion, the two men greeted each other amicably. There was no room for differences. At such times, you come together, stand together and fight together. Brendan was asked to point out where he believed the most vulnerable areas to be. After several attacks, he knew exactly where the criminals were most likely to enter and exit the area. Brendan had spent many nights tracking footprints and chasing intruders. Based on his advice, diagrams were drawn on the map and surveillance positions for each person was charted. Monique was the only woman present. She had
ties to the police force as a weekend warrior. She was the one who had received the Intel about the operating criminals responsible for most of the attacks in that sector.

She took the lead at the meeting and explained the plan of action. "Everyone is assigned a position," she explained. "You are not to move from there under any circumstances. This is how we stay safe. We want to avoid any accidents." Monique was a tough, hardened woman, with broad shoulders, who could handle a brawl like any man. She knew how to take care of herself. "There, where you are allocated, you sit and you wait. When you see someone, you fire. No questions asked. That is why no-one is to move from where they are positioned. Warn your farm workers to stay inside their houses tonight. There shouldn't be a single person walking around at that time. Those who are will be the ones who are up to no good; the savages that are coming for us. We'll wait them out. Tonight, we will fight back. When I give the signal, collect your shotgun shells and return home. No one is to speak of this again."

Everyone nodded in agreement. Desperation had driven them insane. Brendan explained that he could not take part because of his responsibility at the lodge, but would warn them if he suspected activity, or would go and help if something went wrong. At 2am that night, the first shot was fired. The painfully loud, thumping noise jolted my heart within the rib cage of my chest. I felt overwhelmed by the conflicting emotions of both fear and sadness. About fifty more thunderous cracks, with short intervals in-between, followed like fireworks on Guy Fawkes Night. I listened with a beating heart, at a chain reaction of gunfire, as the assailants crossed through each farmer's area. By force of will, my inner being remained resilient and invulnerable to the ordeal for a period, but later my sanity deteriorated, like the sea over time wears away at a rock. Nobody can remain unchanged under such relentless and ongoing conditions. Some delinquents have chosen to take the law into their own hands. It is like poking at a beehive. They have turned into ignorant, hateful killers, acting primitively on their desperation. They have become driven and addicted to violence and their hatred has become loudly vocalised. Hatred runs deep and cold within the veins of our society and it is further fuelled by politicians, for their own gain and political agendas. They have chosen to ignore the lessons that we have been taught by the history of other African countries. Violence is rife and common in the youth, and hatred encouraged. Privileged, guarded civilians judge and make liberation speeches about their 'disadvantaged past' and about 'erasing painful reminders' from behind their castle walls, while educational institutions go up in flames and memorial buildings are violently burned to the ground. Intelligent thinkers recognise it as merely an excuse for poor behaviour and a manipulation of our sad history in order to receive special treatment. Yes, there were many mistakes made in the history of our country. A regime was in place under which many suffered appallingly. But those wrongdoings were perpetrated by a previous generation. We can only be responsible for our present and future and, as a nation, take actions to rise above the painful reminders of the past. "Two wrongs do not make a right," I was once told and it has stayed with me. We can never correct anything with hateful acts. I believe more people are suffering presently than ever before. We are living in a time where we have all adopted a culture of violence, in one way or the other. Violence feeds off of violence, spreading through the land like burning fire, destroying everything in its way.

CHAPTER 24

"My father-in-law is gearing up for a civil war," Gwyneth says. We are sitting at her kitchen table. Her Glock Z88 pistol is placed within close reach next to her on the table, mere inches away from her grasp. It is an artistic, wood table, positioned in the centre of the kitchen, with four neatly-placed chairs around it. The kitchen walls are painted lime-green and adorned with old and rusted implements, some of which were picked up on the farm and some that were procured from antique shops. She inherited the firearm from her grandmother. It was a lengthy and difficult process to get it licensed in her name, but with the amount of time that Martin is away on projects and she is alone on the farm with the two boys and a third on the way, she couldn't take the chance of being unarmed. It was just one of those things she had to get done. For her birthday, Martin will buy her a shotgun. An unusual gift for a dainty woman like Gwyneth, but we all crave our safety and adjust and adapt ourselves to attain it.

One night before she had her pistol, she was alone at home with the kids when some criminals tried to break through her security gate over the kitchen door at the back of her house. Martin had installed a siren with a button for her to press in case of an emergency. When Gwyneth sounded the alarm, Brendan hurtled on foot towards her house. As fortune would have it, he was patrolling in the nearby vicinity at that very moment. Their barking dogs made him suspicious. He ran through the field, jumped the fence and was there within minutes. When she phoned, he was already surveying any hide-out spots around her house. He saw three men fleeing the property, but he was too late to pursue them. Instead, Brendan brought Gwyneth and the boys back to our farm, carrying the youngest the full distance through the thick bush, where they waited for Martin to return from site.

"They have stockpiled tinned food and bottles of water. They are getting paranoid and are worried that total anarchy will break out. I suppose they feel vulnerable on the farm because of their old age. My mother-in-law is constantly checking the news and social media. All the violent stories they read about is traumatic to them," Gwyneth explains, while slowly sipping her coffee.

"Sadly, not even the old and defenceless are spared," I add. "I understand their distress. Fortunately, I don't think we are facing a war. The frequent attacks just have us all a little paranoid. And then there is all the talk of politicallymotivated propaganda advocating white genocide in the country."

Martin had invited us over for a braai. The two men are outside chatting around the braai. The topic of crime, and especially farm attacks, always came up in conversation. We couldn't get around
it. It was like it owned us as slaves to its incumbency.

"Martin and I sleep in shifts now. We don't dare to both be asleep at the same time. One of us is always awake, listening, making sure that no one is trying to get inside. I'm tired, Danelle. Will this ever end?"

We met up with Gwyneth and Martin at least twice a week for dinner, or lunch, or even just a quick cup of coffee. Gwyneth and I took turns to drive the kids to and from school.
Some days Gwyneth would treat us to a feast of delicious home-cooked traditional foods, prepared in the large coal stove that was an antique feature in her farmhouse kitchen. We spent hours in each other's company. Our lifestyles were our common ground and our friendship grew from there. We understood each other's fear and torment. We were plagued and bound by the same set of circumstances.

Talking to Gwyneth provided the solace I needed for encouragement. I was ready to give up. Many nights I soaked my pillow in tears, too tired to move, but too afraid to fall asleep. I lay motionless, as salty drops of water ran down my nose and cheeks. We had placed the farm on the market, but in eleven months hadn't yet found a single interested buyer. Our entire life's work and savings were tied up in the farm. The dream that we'd once had had soon turned into a nightmare. I remembered Roger's eagerness to sign the agreement, to let the place go. And his ailing health.

With the harshness of our environment, my gentle heart became hardened. I hated the world for the way it had changed me, but even more so I hated my new self. When I looked in the mirror, I no longer recognised who I saw there. My skin had turned grey and my eyes had lost their youthful sparkle. The scar I got when we fled the house the night of the attack, runs down the centre of my forehead as a painful reminder. My hair had become dry and coarse, and carelessly framed my dreary-looking face. There was not a smidgeon left of my former buoyant spirit. There was only the ghost of that person staring back at me. I mourned her loss. I don't know how to be strong without becoming hard. It made me depressed. At times, it felt like I was fighting an inner war, too - against myself and my senseless, over-exaggerated fear that imprisoned me. In this struggle, it was only me against the world. I cried in the shower under the running water, biting down on my hand to muffle the self-pitying sobs. I couldn't let the kids or Brendan see what I felt. A mother needs to stay composed. She is the heartbeat of the family. The glue that bonds all the components together. I look at other mothers, each of whom, like a mother goose, seems to know how to keep her goslings in an organised row. It looks so natural and easy to them. It makes me feel like a complete failure. And like the leading actress in my life story, I sometimes feel like an imposter who pretends to have it all together. The truth is that the human mind is a very lonely place. Although you try as you may through conversation to allow someone to enter your thoughts, you are never able to show someone your mind in its entirety, to completely invite them in. People may see the outer, physical presentation of who you are, but there is a whole other dimension that is practically invisible. I have always carried the weakness of being an idealist, who believes in the possibility of a perfect world, a place where people live in peace and have tranquil lives, filled with carefree days. Instead, my heart was racing through life like a derailed train. It is unrealistic, foolish even, but it is the reason why this life is slowly killing me. I was not made resilient enough to fight this emotional struggle; I spend my life in endless fear. It is like I'm waiting for my heartbeats to run out. I used to believe that I had complete control over my mind; the way I viewed the world around me and how I fit into that picture. Suddenly, however, I found myself in a very dark place. Other people's lives seemed so simple. I stared at them as if through a glass wall. That life, the one they lived, was unattainable to me. And yet, in a strange way I had never wished for it either, for I could not be who they were.

We spent our lives protecting owls, but who would protect us? As I sit down at my computer, I curiously open onto Facebook. I no longer have the nerve to pick up a newspaper; journalists only seem to find bad news to report on. The first post at the top of my timeline reads: "Mother of three murdered in Hartbeespoort." My heart leaps in my chest. I carry on reading. I know I shouldn't. It serves no purpose to know about it, but for some reason my curiosity won't leave it alone. It is not someone I know, but my devastation remains intense. The article continues to explain the sad scenario of young children waiting for their mother to pick them up from school, as she had done every other day, but on that particular day she hadn't arrived. A family friend had waited at the school with the kids for their mother to come and when an hour had passed and there was no answer on her phone, she had loaded them in her car and driven them home. There, these three young children had found their mother stabbed and bleeding out on the kitchen floor. She had three stab wounds to her neck and another few to her chest. She had lain there slaughtered for her kids to find. She had left the kitchen door open while she'd sat working at her kitchen table. The man she had employed as a gardener had invited his friend over. They'd seen the open door as an opportunity to rob her of her things and then had cold-bloodedly murdered her so that she wouldn't be able to testify against the man she had known and trusted, a man for whom she had provided a job. Her cellphone and laptop, along with some insignificant items, were later found in the possession of the gardener and his accomplice. A friend of the deceased wrote a comment underneath the morbid article that read: "Had he only instead sat down with her at that kitchen table (where he took her life) to learn how she uplifted herself out of poverty. How she built a life for herself and her kids despite her troubled background; he would have left inspired, like she inspired so many others, with a new discovered lease on life." Instead, he had killed and robbed her of what she had worked her whole life to achieve. Her kids had been left orphaned.

The tears well up in my eyes. I mourn for a soul I have never met. I sit weeping over three innocent children who must face the world alone now. They have been robbed of a loving mother to look after them and to guide them through their lives, a mother to kiss them goodnight and pack them lunch each school day. I grieve because I know her fear, the emotions she felt as she slowly and painfully left this world, her worry for those she was leaving behind. It leaves me heavy-hearted and impaired. I struggle to find the strength inside myself to look past the pain in the world.

I have become petrified of life itself and the monsters with whom we share our world.

I shivered every time the phone rang in the early morning hours. It almost always held bad news at the other end. Brendan hardly ever came to bed before 4am. He spent his nights patrolling the farm, looking for intruders, wandering aimlessly with a flashlight. It was soul-destroying. A lonely duty. He would sleep for only three hours before starting his day. This he would spend driving to rescue owls, climbing up ladders and in trees and putting up Owl Houses. He had made it his lifemission to save and protect owls and wouldn't let anything get in the way of that.

When the tiredness set in, his mind would play tricks on him and a few mishaps almost occurred because of the paranoia. On one such occasion, it was just after 1am in the morning when he heard screaming coming from tent six. He approached slowly, brimming with excitement to finally catch the perpetrators red-handed. Adrenaline was pumping through his body. He was about to pull open the flap of the tent, armed and ready to defend the innocent, when he stopped to listen again and realised that the "distressed" screams he thought he'd heard were, rather, moans of pleasure. Instead of facing persecution, the couple in tent six was simply enjoying their time away together.

At midnight one night, the weather turned stormy and miserable outside so he came to bed early. He crawled in closely next to me, resting his arm on mine and around my waist. His hands and feet were cold as ice. I could feel from the weight of his embrace that he was exhausted. I never slept while he was out. I would lie staring into the darkness, with racing thoughts, a baseball bat or knife in hand. I never knew if I would be able fight off any attackers myself, but convincing myself that I could helped to occupy my mind while he was out. I would imagine different scenarios playing out. How I would swing straight at their heads when they tried to climb through the window. How I would hide the knife patiently and strike at just the right moment – an unexpected moment that would give me an advantage point. Thinking this way empowered me to feel brave, rather than defenceless.

Brendan had been in bed for barely twenty-five minutes, but was fast asleep after five, when the phone rang. I had to give him a good shake to wake him. By then, the wind had calmed and it was quiet outside. A hysterical guest was on the phone. They were booked into one of the Log Cabins. They had still been awake, drinking and noisy, when Brendan had come to bed. Their belongings had been stolen from their cabin while they'd been outside, sitting around the fire. It must have happened only minutes after Brendan had left. When he'd passed their cabin earlier, there'd been no sign of any intrusion. He could always tell by the prints in the sand whether someone had been there or not. There had been a few shoe prints that he had come to know well and knew to look out for, ones that belonged to frequently visiting trespassers. When he'd checked their cabin, there'd been nothing but the usual trails left by small animals or insects, a rabbit footprint or shongololo line. Brendan rose to his feet, got dressed and was at their cabin within minutes.

I anticipated another day of anguish. No matter how helpful we tried to be, or what we did or what we said, there was nothing that could salvage the situation. Nobody ever accepted a robbery as an unavoidable, unfortunate incident. They almost always blamed us for it. Some, in a fit of anger or rage, even accused us of the deed ourselves. There was always screaming, shouting and swearing. Demands and threats. They acted as if they didn't live in the same country, or were still naïve about the actuality of crime. It was denial, that's all it was. When we spoke to them, they would tell us that they had all been robbed before, but would not accept it at a place where they had come to have a holiday. It is human nature to seek someone to blame. Because we were a lodge where people came to have a vacation, they had imagined, for some reason, that we would be immune to the prevailing crime and violent attacks that were taking place everywhere else in the country. Phoning the cops to come out was nothing but a futile exercise. They were rude and uninterested. They never did anything more than open a docket that would be added to thousands of other case files that never received attention, or were even investigated. It was more for insurance purposes than anything else that we called them, and our professional protocol to be helpful. If the guest had insurance, they would need the case number to claim.

One day, the local police picked up a criminal from our premises, drove him a few kilometres up the road and dropped him off again. He was back on our farm with two others that same night. Brendan spotted them and chased them passed the tents, through thick thorn bushes, to the fence where they had made a large hole earlier that evening, big enough to drive a car through. From there, they disappeared again into the night. To search any further would be pointless; it was like trying to find a needle in a haystack. The police officers knew him by name. The spoor he left was unmistakable. It wasn't recognisable because of the shoes he wore. Those were common sneakers. It was the noticeable print left by the protruding big toe of his right foot that stuck through a hole in the sole of his shoe. You would think that with all the cellphones, all the laptops and tablets he stole and peddled, that he would replace his broken shoes, but he never did. It was almost like a proud trademark that he left behind. A taunting game of cat and mouse. He was responsible for about a quarter of the criminal activity on the farms in the area.

There were many other opportunistic, nightlurking offenders like him, wandering around like zombies, hoping to stumble upon unsuspecting victims. Catching one wouldn't make much difference. There were hundreds of thousands more of the same calibre people prowling in the darkness. Each night, invariably, someone is attacked, robbed, murdered or raped in their home somewhere in the country. There was nothing unique about our situation; this is many peoples' reality. Some families have experienced things so horrific that the shadow of darkness they have cast over their lives will never entirely leave them. They could tell stories that would make me feel ashamed about my self-pity. Innocent families are callously killed, or tortured to death. We have been the lucky ones; so far, we somehow have managed to escape this unthinkable fate each time.

After two further attempts by robbers trying to break into Martin and Gwyneth's home, Gwyneth finally broke down one day during one of our chats. Her eyes teared up as she expressed her desperation for an exit plan. She had, in moments of sheer desperation, walked out in her garden and fired several shots from her handgun in a despairing plea to abolish any further threat to her family. She became conscious of her actions moments later and had to accept that she is powerless in this battle. I recognised the same onset of depression in her as I did in myself.

By the time Albert and his wife were robbed, the whole scene had played out like a theatrical spell in front of my eyes. Everyone was roleplaying, like characters in a play. Each reaction was unoriginally predictable. The recurring crimes left us with a moral dilemma. When considering the potential danger that the situation could bring, we decided to close the lodge to the public until we had managed to guarantee the safety of visiting guests. Brendan and I had spoken about closing up often and had considered it many times before, but now we no longer saw any other way forward. People's lives could be in danger. The thought tormented us. The lodge was closed for about three months, while we sought to employ a private security company to supply guards to patrol throughout the nights.

Later we would employ an anti-poaching team. Besides the guests, the owls and the animals were also at risk. Owls sell for about R500 a head on the black market, bought by witchdoctors for traditional medicines and spells. It is believed that consuming some of the parts of the body will bring you wisdom, or that you could bring death to another with the body of an owl. Snares were removed on a weekly basis. We installed camera traps and considered other technology, like a security drone, to safeguard the area. We tried everything in our power to make the place safe, but nothing would stop the criminals from coming. They are drawn to it like ants to sugar. There is plenty of bait, new fresh victims to ransack every night. It is a disaster area, with a violent culture, and they will continue to plunder. But we couldn't give up. It would have not only meant our own downfall, but it would also force the closure of the rescue centre. Without the funding of the lodge, we would not be able to afford to look after the owls any longer and the Centre, a cause we have passionately built up over about a decade of hard work and effort, would be shut down. We could lose the property and would have no place to carry on with the rehabilitation work. Every person in our employment would lose their livelihood and their homes. Is it fair to give up something that you have worked so hard to obtain because of others' selfish acts? Because of uncivilised thugs? Where will it end? Without another option of income, the lodge was opened again with the new security measures in place. We didn't know what challenges would lie ahead of us, but I knew one thing for sure - the situation was like a ticking bomb; one day it would blow up and there would be nothing left to salvage.

It was quiet for almost three weeks and we were convinced that our security efforts had finally paid off … before the worst possible scenario happened. A school group of twelve learners spent a weekend at the Centre, on an educational camp for their biology class. They were all city kids and a few of them had never been on a farm before, or experienced the great outdoors. They excitedly explored the environment and we had a full schedule planned for the two days and two nights they would spend learning about conservation. After a long day of hiking up the mountain, they returned to camp to settle in for the night. It was the beginning of autumn and although the days were still hot, the nights had a crisp chill in the air. Some sat around the fire, while others were getting ready to crawl into bed. Themba was the securityguard appointed to watch over them for the night. He was in a discussion with the two teachers when he excused himself to do a quick check around the back of the dormitory, where the learners were housed, and to check along the fence line for any sign of an intrusion. He was away for mere seconds when three men entered the camp, one armed with a gun, one with a knife and another with a machete. The men ordered the students to the ground, robbed them of their belongings and disappeared again. Brendan was already en route when he received the call. He was halfway there to do one of his routine checks. Our young recruits took the students to safety and the chase, which was later joined by every farmer in a twenty-kilometre radius, began. The area was blocked off and about fifty angry people were all waiting to bring the perpetrators to justice. Sniffer dogs were used to follow the scent. But they had vanished, as if into thin air. This is when Brendan realised that they had had help; someone was hiding them. He followed their footprints to the fence, where he noticed that they had met up with other footprints from the next-door farm. As the two sets of footprints met up on each side of the fence and had come from opposite directions, as revealed in the sand, he could determine that a conversation had taken place between the men. He confronted the hired security-guard from the neighbouring farm, who claimed that someone had come to the fence asking for a glass of water. An unlikely explanation. With a bit of pressure and threats that he would be linked to the crimes, he gave up the guilty parties. Brendan now had names of the suspects. Over the next few days, he started asking around. Two days later, his phone rang. One of the guys was willing to talk, if offered a reward for the information. He said that one of the suspects - the one who had carried the firearm in the robbery and was also believed to be the main instigator - was strolling along the gravel road, directly across from our farm, on the opposite side of the tar road, with two of his accomplices. It looked like troops who was gearing up for an attack on an army base, as our young recruits scattered to get organised. Brendan, the recruits and Martin got into the vehicles and rushed to catch the guys who were responsible for an armed robbery on twelve young students. Martin and Gwyneth were having coffee with us when the information came through. Martin set out to help Brendan, while the women gathered to safeguard our children. For a moment, I felt like I was transported back in time to a place of war. It was like I was feeling empathy for those who had lived before me and for the battles they had to fight. Brendan didn't have much of a description to go on, other than the white-coloured pants and the shoes a man known as Tshepho Moya was wearing. He followed the man who he believed was Tshepho to an illegitimate bar, or "shebeen" as it is called here in Africa, about five kilometres from our farm. A man with light pants came outside, but was wearing the wrong shoes. Brendan followed the road down to the informal settlement to see what he could find. He had Peterson with him in his vehicle. When they came back, the man was still outside the shebeen, curiously asking if they had tracked the guy that they were looking for. Brendan had a polite discussion with the man, who had introduced himself as 'Simon'. Simon was very willing to share information. He said that he knew Tshepho and the trouble he always caused. He said that Tshepho had recently been released from jail. He had received a three-year sentence for armed robbery, but was out on parole, after only a year. Simon seemed eager to share his knowledge of the band of robbers. He claimed to be a police informant. The next day, Brendan passed Simon again and slowed down to talk to him. As Simon saw Brendan approaching he turned and ran, jumping through a razor-wire fence. Later that day, Brendan learned that Simon was in fact, Tshepho and had played him all along. The armed robbery was reported to the police and a case was opened, but the detective never bothered to pitch up for an investigation. Brendan had gathered all the information necessary for an arrest, but the corrupt police force was uninterested.

CHAPTER 25

We were on our way back from a project when Bryan phoned about Frank. When I'd spoken to Kerry the day before, she'd mentioned that Frank hadn't left his room for two days. The Landy's engine cranked and rumbled in my ears as we drove through the quiet Karoo and it was hard to make out exactly what Bryan was explaining to me over the phone. I asked Brendan to pull over to the side of the road for a moment, so that I could hear him more clearly. Kerry and Bryan had become concerned about Frank's ailing condition. They suspected a stroke.

"Take him to a doctor, we will pick up the account," I instructed. "Let us know what the Doc says. You can't take any chances with something serious like this. We'll be home a little later tonight."

As I ended the call, I felt a hollow and uneasy sensation travelling through my body and a nauseous feeling creeping up into my throat. It was a Wednesday and the gravity of the week still lay ahead like a mountain in front of me. There was always something that needed to be dealt with. The previous Sunday, Kerry had phoned just before 6pm, after returning from the pub with Bryan, to let me know that we had been robbed again. All the bedding had been stolen from the tents. Kerry's laptop was also missing from her room and Bryan had lost a few items, too. Frank had been the only person on the farm at the time, but Frank was seemingly unaware of the incident. He had been in bed when they'd returned and had told Kerry the following morning that he was not feeling well. She'd suspected that he had the flu and thought he would feel better in a day or two. On the Wednesday morning, after Frank hadn't left his room for days, Kerry and Bryan had gone into Frank's room to check on him. The staircase to his room was covered in vomit. This is when Bryan had phoned me.

Bryan later came back with more news. "The doctor suspects a stroke, but wants to send him for tests. Kerry is taking him to the District Public Hospital. He asked me to phone his brother." Bryan then quoted Frank's plea to him: "'I'm no longer any good to anyone. Please ask my brother to come and fetch me.' That's the only thing I could make out. He is very disorientated," Bryan said. "I'll take care of it. I'll locate his brother to
inform him of Frank's condition."

It took me a few hours to find contact information for Frank's only living relatives, a half-brother who lived in England with his wife Jenny. I managed to find Frank's sister-in-law on Facebook and sent her a message. At that stage, we knew little about Frank's condition, but I knew that he would need the support of everyone close to him. His words to Bryan deeply saddened me; no person should ever feel worthless. At 7pm, we were still on the road. I phoned Kerry back to ask about Frank. There had been little change since our last conversation and they were still sitting in the hospital waiting room, waiting for a doctor to attend to him. The room was filled with sick and injured people. Some had bleeding stab wounds and some were hardly conscious, but they were all unsympathetically left sitting there, like leper sufferers who were pushed out of society, their condition believed to be a punishment from God himself. They say money can't buy everything, but here money would buy sympathy. You only had to compare the difference in public medical care to private care to know this. Paramedics rushed in with more emergency patients every passing hour. The hospital is understaffed and the nurses and hospital personnel who are there, have become callous and immune to the suffering that goes on around them. Through seeing and experiencing so much pain and agony, they've had to disassociate themselves from normal human emotion and have lost their compassion and value for life or death in the process. Kerry and Frank had been waiting in the same hall for the past five hours. It was packed with rows and rows of uncomfortable plastic chairs. There was a security guard who monitored the sliding-door access to the room, where the glass door opening and closing created an annoying sound behind each new patient who entered. Kerry kept glancing up at the wall clock, as if to move it along faster. They waited until 10pm, when Frank's name was called. Finally, a doctor would see him. Frank was sent for testing for poisoning. Something about his symptoms made the doctor suspect the possibility of it and he ordered blood work to be done. Kerry never received the results of this, but assumed that it had turned up negative when they continued with further testing. Later, Frank was transferred to a hospital in Rustenburg. Kerry, kind-hearted and caring as she is, followed the ambulance in her own car. She knew that at that very point in time, she was the only person on this earth who could be there to support Frank.

She stuck closely to the ambulance, travelling in the dark to an unfamiliar place, through unsafe areas, where a woman in her worst nightmare wouldn't want to find herself. But Kerry is selfless and her thoughts were only on Frank. At this hospital, he was taken for a CT scan to determine the possibility of brain damage. The test results confirmed a brain haemorrhage. The doctor's initial conclusion was that the bleeding had been brought on by a head trauma - a possible hard blow to the head - but he couldn't say for sure. The blood could have come from a stroke, caused by a burst artery, which would then have resulted in localised bleeding in the surrounding tissue. There was a set of stairs in his cottage that he had to climb up to get to his room, or down to get to the bathroom. He could have slipped, fallen and hit his head on the edge of the wooden steps. Or, he could have interrupted the burglars on Sunday. They could have hit him over the head with a blunt object. Or, alternatively, the cause was a common stroke. Frank had no memory of anything that had happened over those past few days and couldn't provide any clarity on the matter. When he spoke, it was mostly mumbling. At 2am, Frank was finally admitted and given a hospital bed in which to lie down. When Kerry asked him about how he felt, he answered under his breath that he was very tired. She told him to get some sleep. She promised to return early the next morning with some fresh clothes and toiletries. She left Frank in Ward 9, Bed 4, of Joe Shimankana Tabane Hospital in Rustenburg, and drove for an hour to get back home. She left our contact numbers with the hospital, should there be any reason to get hold of us. We served as his next of kin in his otherwise solitary existence. There was talk from the doctor that he might have to operate to relieve some of the pressure, but the hospital would contact us should this be the case.

I saw Kerry for the first time, after returning from our project, at 7am on Thursday morning. She had a perplexed and distressed expression on her face. I made her a cup of coffee and asked if she had managed to gather some toiletries and clothes for Frank. "Yes," she answered, "the bag is all packed and ready, but I cannot find Frank." Kerry had been up all night worrying about him. They had grown very close over the past year. Frank was always willing to listen and Kerry likes to talk. Kerry phoned the hospital and they informed her that Frank had been transferred to a state hospital in Pretoria.

When she phoned the hospital in Pretoria, they told her that Frank had been transferred back to Rustenburg, but this hospital maintained that they had no patient by that name. The very idea of a hospital misplacing a patient seemed improbable to me. I started phoning frantically, still covertly believing that Kerry was confused and that lack of sleep was a probable reason for her misconception. Every time I was given the same answer. "There is no patient by the name Frank in this hospital."

"F-R-A-N-K F-A-R-R-A-R B-O-C-K," I spelled it out. "There must be some record or file on him. Please can you help me?"

I phoned the hospital in Pretoria again, where the person I spoke to insisted that he had been transferred back to Rustenburg. Somewhere in the muddle of several telephone conversations, I was given two other public state hospitals to check in Rustenburg and Pretoria, respectively. The hospital in Rustenburg later told me that he had been transferred to Brits District Hospital, but this hospital said that they had no record of him whatsoever. I phoned again and again. Frank was lost somewhere between five state hospitals and no matter how many times I tried, I couldn't find out anything about his whereabouts or his condition. Each time I phoned, I took a different approach. I begged, I pleaded and I threatened. I phoned Ward 9, where Kerry had left Frank in the early morning hours.

A hard-hearted nurse answered the phone: "Ma'am, I need your help," I started. "I'm looking for an old man who was admitted to your ward earlier this morning. We want to bring him clean clothes to put on and toiletries to wash up. Please can you confirm that he is there?" I pretended, for my own sanity mostly, that I hadn't been trying for the last three hours to get an answer to the very same question. "His name is Frank Farrar Bock. He is an old man and must be wondering where we are."

Without a word to me, I could hear her, in the background, shouting down the hall in an African language with which I was not familiar, to whom I assumed were the other nurses in the same ward. The only thing that I could make out from what she was saying was Frank's name - not his full name either, only "Frank." A conversation ensued amongst them. Although I didn't understand anything of the conversation in which I was not included, something about the tone in which they conversed made me believe that they knew him. This provided temporary relief and made me take a deep breath in anticipation. I felt powerless over the matter and was at a point of utter desperation.

Frank's name was mentioned a few more times, before she came back on the line: "There is no Frank here." My shoulders dropped in dreary hopelessness.

"But if he is not there, please can you tell me what is written in his file. There must be some way that you can help me?"

"There is no file here for Frank. Frank is not here," she answered indifferently.

I phoned the hospital operator again to check the other wards. Later, I got hold of a training doctor who had just came on duty. His voice sounded young and I was hopeful that he would take more interest in my entreaty. I pleaded with him to check each ward for me, hoping that his compassion for saving lives and moral obligation to a fellow human-being were still intact. Still no information turned up. Just before 8pm on that Thursday evening, I gave up my quest to find Frank this way. Emotionally exhausted, I returned to the boma fire where everyone else was gathered. The feeling of bitter frustration lingered in me, creating a heaviness in my limbs. We agreed to personally go and look for him the following morning. We would drive from hospital to hospital and check each ward and each bed ourselves.

Brendan's phone rang at 4am on Friday morning. I woke up straight away. It was completely silent around us, which meant that I could hear every word spoken by the person on the other end of the conversation.

"Do you know Frank?" the female voice asked Brendan.

"Yes, yes, is he there? We have been looking for him. Which hospital are you phoning from?"

She was phoning from the hospital in Rustenburg, where they had told me repeatedly that Frank was not a patient there. I lay motionless, listening.
"Frank passed away." That is all she said. Brendan thanked her for her phone call and hung up.

Frank had died all alone, in a hard and uncomfortable hospital bed, with only strangers around. I couldn't help feeling miserable about this. What if he had thought, in his final hour of need, that there was no one out there who had cared enough to visit? That Kerry had broken her promise. He would never know how hard we had tried to find him. How desperately I had wanted to see him and remind him that we did care. And that he did matter to someone in this life. He mattered to us. He lived a solitary life and in the time that we knew him, no one ever came to see him on the farm, but he had many stories to tell and he was a good listener. I remembered, with fondness, the numerous conversations we'd had. He was a philosopher and had a vast knowledge of politics and social sciences. We liked the same music. I had told him about the book I was writing and he was eager to read it, but never got the opportunity to do so. A week after Frank's passing, professed friends arrived from Rustenburg like famished vultures to take claim of his world possessions.

His treasures, by which he measured his worth in this world, were picked up, tossed around and snatched up by scavenger treasure hunters. In the years he had lived with us, they hadn't spared a single moment to visit him, but in his exit from this life, they had hurried over to gain from his death. Rest in peace, Frank. The world is a cruel, cruel place. May your soul live happy wherever you may find yourself now.

CHAPTER 26

When I was younger, I used to read the first three chapters of a new book before skipping to the final chapter. The initial three, opening chapters would give me a good indication of whether or not I liked the way the story was going, but then I would have an itching urge to uncover whether it would end well, before continuing with it. I suppose, like any typical idealist, I wanted to know that I could look forward to a happy ending for the characters in the book, because the uncertainty and suspense was otherwise too much to bear. Often, I had hoped to fast forward through my own life to know the purpose towards which it is ultimately moving. Wouldn't it be easier to make the right decisions then? Maybe if I knew what I could expect out of life, I would know to spend my time more wisely. I dream of being able one day to go to sleep without worrying about being woken by the violence of an attack; without lying only partially asleep, with my hand placed strategically on a weapon of self defense; and without being locked up inside a prison cell of sorts but, instead, to go to sleep in peace, with the freedom that only safety can provide. I dream of a quiet, tranquil little home with a scenic view, without cavernous high walls that casts dark shadows over my soul, cutting razor wire, electric fencing and incarcerating burglar bars. I dream to be able to live and let live, and to just be … and for my free-spirited self to once more dance with the spirits of the wind and of the sea … and to paint in the colours of the rainbow.

In conversation, I have often heard people say: "What will happen to this country of ours? Will we still have a place in it? What future will our children have?" I have often wondered the same thing. Will the violence subside? Will we become more tolerant of one another? Or will our country erupt into war and, like a volcano, finally break through to the surface. If so, will we make it out in time? In the meantime, one-byone, the farmlands are being invaded and people are being mowed down like grass with a scythe.

When I was a child, I suffered from the same recurring nightmare. It started shortly after the armed robbery. Night after night, I would dream of an army of faceless, dark men, rising from the shadows on the horizon. They would approach with scorching flames and I, along with my family, would be trapped in the centre of their evil circle
of rage. I would wake in a panic as they drew nearer and nearer and there would be an upsurge of wicked flames, as if we were about to burn in hell itself. The nightmare returned to me in more recent days, which caused me considerable anxiety. My fears had reached such intensity that it had an adverse effect on my health, especially on my heart. It became difficult for me to distinguish between the physical threats and those that lived in my thoughts and prevailed over my sanity. "Have faith," they say - faith in God, faith in yourself and faith in the greater good. But faith in itself cannot change the physical world. What it can change is our perception of the world. I had to believe that things were not really as bad as I was making them out

to be; that the world was not out to harm me, but that we'd only had a run of bad luck through the choices we had made in our lives.

In my life, I have often wondered about luck - good or bad. I maintain an unusual balance between the two. However unlucky I have felt, or however often bad luck has struck, I have not been able to help but notice my good luck at the same time, too. When I started my studies in the field of Psychology, it was to find answers to help me better understand human behaviour. For example, what happens to individuals during certain stages of their lives that makes them commit deeds that are so unthinkable and so cruel? In later years, after completing my studies, people have often asked me: "Have you found the answers to your questions? Do you understand now?"

I believe in not judging a person's behaviour, but to judge the intentions behind the behaviour, instead. Brendan once caught a guy who was stealing from us. Instead of pressing charges and having him locked up, which in this country is worse than the death sentence, we decided to help him. Brendan asked me to talk to him. We believed that he probably hadn't intended to cheat and to deceive us, but that there must have been a bigger reason for what he was caught doing. The man was an employee who had approached us for work a few months before. He had walked in off the street. At the time, he had been sharing a wood house with five relatives and had no money even for food. We offered him accommodation, food and a salary enough to live on. I liked him straight away. He carried a

depth of both innocence and pain in his eyes. Even for a broken world-worn man, he seemed driven and willing to work. When
I asked him why he had done what he did, he
teared up and asked if it would be possible for him ever to regain our trust. Out of desperation brought on by an addiction, he had sold a long list of items, such as the tools and equipment he had been given to work with, to the pawn shops in the area. With his name and identity number, Brendan was able to retrieve this list as evidence against him.

Once, when a bird I had cared for deeply passed away, he found me in a very vulnerable state. He came running over to see if I was alright. This stuck with me and I would never forget the kindness he had shown. We took a walk to a quiet spot, where a wood table with benches was positioned under large marula trees. I asked him what events had led up to where he was then. He seemed willing to talk unreservedly about his past. He told me that he had been seven years of age when his mother had decided to leave his father. His father, who had come to hear about this, had then loaded him, along with his older brother, in the car for 'a short little drive', but they had never returned home. His father had kidnapped his sons to punish his wife for wanting to leave. His dad was a violent man, who had assaulted and abused them in many ways. The school they attended
soon realised that both the boys had black-andblue marks spread across their small little bodies. Their legs resembled bruised bananas. They were placed into foster care which,

according to him, wasn't any better. Throughout his life he felt worthless, unloved and rejected. Despite this, he was still determined to make something of himself. He gained a scholarship as a talented rugby player and managed to complete his secondary education, while living in a boarding school. In his early twenties, he managed to get himself a good job and a place to stay. He met a girl whom he planned to marry. She fell pregnant and a baby girl, named Diana, was born. When Diana was three months old, he arrived home one day from work to find a letter on the dressing-table. His fiancé was gone. She was too young to deal with the relationship and the responsibility and had gone on the run with her mother, who was going through a divorce, and they had taken Diana with them. This was the second biggest disappointment he had to face in his life, the first being that his mother had never tried to find them. To numb his inconsolable feelings and to escape this new reality, he had become involved with drugs. It was then five years down the line when he'd had to steal from us to support this ongoing habit.

Between us, we came up with an arrangement. He agreed to work to pay for what he had taken. He would be given food and a place to stay, but would have no access to money and wouldn't be allowed to go anywhere without supervision. He has remained clean ever since and, in due time, his normal work privileges and conditions were restored. We spoke often and I helped him to work through some of what he was feeling. I also promised to help him find his little girl.

But not all stories end with a happy-ever-after. The truth is that the human psyche is so complex and so diverse that I don't believe one definitive answer can ever be found. The psyches of some people are simply a knotty mess of evil and malicious viciousness, so much so that it would never be possible to untangle them to the point where they could be understood. Is it hurt, or is it pure evil that feeds the fire of violence? My heart bleeds for a country I both love and loathe.

I was excited when Brendan suggested a research project on Cape Eagle Owls in the Outeniqua and Tsitsikamma forests. Although he never said it in so many words, I suspected that he, too, sought freedom from the effects that such a hostile environment casts over you. The brief escape was reason enough to take on a project based over a thousand kilometres away. We had done extensive work with many of the other species, but there was little research available on the Cape Eagle Owl which, in our projects thus far, had been an elusive bird. We had great expectations of compiling comprehensive information on our field research and then filming and piecing it together in a wildlife documentary. Our knowledge on urban owls was vast and comprehensive, but our information on species in the wilderness areas was still incomplete. We'd had countless successes with our projects in our direct areas, but wished to extend this across the country. We set off on an eleven-month research project that would lead us to the Western coastline of South Africa. I had packed everything, right down to my last most valuable possession, on the five-foot trailer that we would tow behind the Land

Rover, to a place that would be home for most of the following year. It would be a full two-day trip to get there. Bryan, along with nine other staff, would carry on with the normal running of the Centre. Brendan would fly up once a month, for a week at a time, to action any important projects and to oversee the releases of already rehabilitated owls. Even though I realised that it was not going to be a permanent move, I felt conflicted by the uncertainty of splitting my life into two. I didn't want to leave anything behind, in case it got stolen before our return, but it seemed silly to pack everything when we would be gone only for a short while. Everything but furniture was packed into large, plastic, storage containers and loaded onto the trailer. Even my vast collection of books and art supplies, which no home invaders would have any interest in stealing, was packed up. There was a small part inside me that secretly hoped to pack up and never return. I longed to live a simple and uncomplicated life. That was the whole idea anyway, when we had first decided to open an animal rehabilitation centre. I'm not sure where it had all become such a big mess, or when I had started suffering from depression. My only tie to the place remained the owls, which was connected to my childlike heart and the belief that it was my purpose and responsibility in this life to protect and care for them. I know each owl individually and they are a part of me in the same way that dying is a part of life. It felt like a degree of betrayal to leave - in part to the owls, but also of myself. As we drove through the country, further and further away from a place that was now known as one of the most dangerous places in South Africa, I could slowly feel the tightness in my chest depart, as if evaporating into the clear air. I opened my window wide to breathe in the open air, as if to take new life into my lungs.

We reached the quietness of the Karoo at sunset and, for the first time in a very long time, I embraced the burning-red twilight like a long-lost friend. A vivacious smile danced on my face and I felt like crying out in euphoric bliss. I experienced pre-eminent freedom. Like an owl that had just been released from captivity, I felt like life was waiting for me to live it. For the moment, the Karoo and the Western coast of South Africa still remains unaffected by the epidemic of violent crimes that torment and plague the rest of the land.

The house we rented, located in the quaint little town of Wilderness, was a beautiful, old, threestorey, German-style guest house. It had six bedrooms, four of which we could rent out to travellers to subsidise the cost of the project. The Outeniqua Mountain was its backdrop. The house was located directly opposite the lagoon and, from our bedroom, we had views of both the lagoon and the sea. I soon discovered that there is no better therapist than the untamed sea. When we arrived, I kicked off my shoes and walked barefooted to the beach. My healing process started there, with a long walk on the sand, while the waves crashed into my thoughts. I felt frolicsome as I entered the water. I felt weightless and careless in the mightiness of its force, drifting along without constraint, as my cares were washed away with every crashing wave. There, people still walked the streets, even in darkness, without trepidation. It took us a while to adjust to the idea. We had become so used to living with fear, that we didn't know any better and had accepted it as part of normal life. Like a back pain that you learn to live with, you are always aware of its presence, but adjust to it and eventually it becomes an indistinguishable part of you. This is something that I will not allow for my children. I will not allow them to become conditioned to violence, to accept it as part of ordinary life. I won't succumb to the culture of violence that prevails in our modern society.

As we lay in bed on our first night in a new home, my thoughts couldn't help but wander to the owls that were in the centre. I realised that I wouldn't be there when it was time for them to take their first flight into the wild - a moment in time that carried great sentiment for me. Then, I heard a sound outside that was so inconceivable that I thought that I was dreaming. I ran to the door that led to a staircase to the roof, where I heard it as clear as day. As I turned, I saw the silhouette of a Spotted Eagle Owl, hooting from the far end pitch of our roof. He sat there like an angel; an usher with a message. And I knew that everything would be quite alright. We spent our days hiking through the forest and interviewing people about owl sightings. We hiked up mountains and crawled through caves. On days that we were not busy with the project, we packed a picnic basket, bicycled to the lagoon and sat there bird-watching for the day. On other occasions, we would row a boat up the Touws River, enveloped by jungle-like mountains on either side of us, to where the river finally met up with a waterfall. There we sat, completely at peace with the world, working through hours of recordings. When the weather allowed, we spent our afternoons on the beach; sitting there in a silent stare as the surf washed over the sand or frolicking in the waves. On Saturdays, we supported the local trade by visiting markets where we purchased all our fresh produce.

Our life had been simplified. We hardly ever used a vehicle for travelling and either walked or rode our bicycles to where we wanted to go. This transcendence into a completely new life, gave me the opportunity to recover in order to become myself again, with the kids as the focal-point of my being. Brendan travelled often, returning to the Centre to make sure that the projects were doing well. I used this time, while he was away, to write my book. The life that was still waiting for me to return to, felt like some surreal memory which I had completely detached myself from. On occasion, Brendan would tell me about the electric cables or the water pump that had been stolen from our house. On another trip he told me about the cupboards that had been broken out and that the electricity transformer box had been stolen too. I tried not to let it bring me down for too long and instead focused on where I was. Here, in a quaint little coffee shop in the quiet sea village, I could write my story without fear; knowing that there were miles between myself and my nightmare. Eleven months later, we returned to the Centre to continue with our normal rehabilitation work. I had missed the bush and its simplicity. Spending time outside in the veld, observing the owls on the Sanctuary who had gone through the rehabilitation process and had been released to live freely, makes my life worth living. Brendan and I spend many nights under the starry sky, watching, observing and quietly smiling at the progress in these owls who have graced us with their presence; knowing we've had the fortunate opportunity to share in a part of their life. The more we came to realize the need for the work that we do, the heavier the responsibility weighed on us. For the past decade we have been completely duty-bound to the cause of saving and protecting owls. There is no doubt that our lives are unlike anyone else's in the entire world, spending almost every moment of our time in the familiarity of one owl or the other. Saving owls gives my life a distinct purpose and meaning and I will always consider it a great privilege. In the ten years of living with owls, they have taught me more about life than any other being. The time away had given me time to heal and forget. I had come to know that in the darkest hours of my nights, the owls would always be there, filling up the night sky and watching over us like guardians.

When I reflect back on our life and the experiences that we have lived through, I can't help to feel blessed. Through all the dangerous encounters, we have managed to remain safe and physically unharmed; as if endowed with divine favour. Despite the challenges that we have faced, we have had much more to be grateful for. We spend each day, doing what we are passionate about – living with and caring for owls.

Danelle with two baby Marsh Owls that were rescued from a fire.

Goliath, an emaciated and dehydrated few-day-old Southern White-faced Scops Owlet whom Danelle nursed back to health when he was rescued by the Centre.

Danelle examines the damaged eye of Hedwig, a Spotted Eagle Owl who was hit by a car. Hedwig is now a permanent resident at the Sanctuary and serves as a foster mom to baby owls that are rescued by Owl Rescue Centre.

Danelle feeding baby Barn Owls

A Spotted Eagle Owl photographed on the signboard for Owl Rescue Centre.

Danelle enjoying a visit from a Spotted Eagle Owl, while having a bath in the treehouse bath Brendan built in a Marula tree on the Sanctuary.

Brendan and Danelle on one of their rescue missions. Here, they rescued three orphaned Barn Owls.

Danelle with two Spotted Eagle Owlets she reared when they fell from their nest and was abandoned by the parents. They were cold and weak when Danelle and Brendan picked them up. The owner of the property where the owls had nested, suspecting they were dead, told them to turn around; but Danelle insisted that she checks them out herself. They were successfully released a few months later.

About the Author

Danelle Murray was a 34-year-old, first time author and is now two years older and wiser with this new reprinted publication. She obtained her Bachelor of Arts degree in Human Sciences and Social services, specialised in the professional context through the University of South Africa (UNISA). This is an applied Psychology Degree. She enrolled for the degree in 2007 as a method to cope with a personal traumatic experience, when she and her husband were abducted by armed robbers in January of 2007. She and her husband are the founders of a non-profit organisation named "Owl Rescue Centre", which is concerned with the conservation of all owl species in Southern Africa. She is the Communications Director of the organisation, but also has hands-on involvement in the conservation projects and rehabilitation processes of the owls. Numerous articles of hers, on the topic of owls, have been published in various magazines and newspapers. However, she feels that her most important role in life is to be a good mother to her two beautiful children, Spencer and Rebecca, at the time of publication aged ten and six respectively, who have adopted their unconventional lifestyle in the bush.